A Book of *Blessings*

Large Print

Publications International, Ltd.

Scripture quotations from *The Holy Bible, King James Version*

Images from Shutterstock.com

Louis Weber, CEO
Publications International, Ltd.
8140 Lehigh Avenue
Morton Grove, IL 60053

ISBN: 978-1-63938-891-2

Manufactured in China.

8 7 6 5 4 3 2 1

Contents

Enriching Our Lives

Prayer is just talking to God—sharing our hopes, our dreams, our fears, and our heartaches with the only one who understands us completely. God yearns to be close to us, to be a part of our lives. God wants us to turn to him whenever we feel weak, scared, or alone, and need someone who can help us.

There is no right way to pray. Some of the most beautiful prayers are the most simple in language. Prayers can be whispered, put into song, shouted out to the heavens, or simply said in one's heart. It is always an appropriate time to pray.

We pray whenever we create space in our day to share with God. We pray with our words, but we can also pray without words. For God not only knows our minds, but he sees the depths of our hearts. He sees us as we truly are, so he always knows what we need.

You may wish to spend a few relaxing moments with this book on a hectic day, reading through a prayer or two alone, during a time of quiet. At other times you might need several soothing prayers to ease your weary, troubled mind. In either case, remember that prayer is both an action and an attitude.

Let this book remind you to pause for a moment and know that God is near. In moments of praise and thanksgiving or in moments of hardship and despair, God's Word holds true: "I am with you always." The blessings we receive every day serve as a reminder of this divine promise.

Chapter 1

Love

And now abideth faith, hope, charity, these three; but the greatest of these is charity.

1 Corinthians 13:13

God, it's a quiet day. Help me pause to listen to you, to talk to you, to enjoy your company. Chase away my guilt and shame and fear, and draw me close to your heart. Remind me that no matter what my earthly roles may be, in your presence I am your child, and you care for me more than I could ever imagine. Let me lean against your heart now, Father, and hear it beating with love for me. Amen.

Open wide the window of our spirits,
O Lord, and fill us full of light;
Open wide the door of our hearts,
that we may receive and entertain
thee with all our powers of adoration
and love.

—Christina Rossetti

But I have trusted in thy mercy;
my heart shall rejoice in thy salvation.

Psalm 13:5

Lord above, you look down upon us, and still you love us. When we look down on others, it is because we are angered and cannot see their points of view. We also still love them, but sometimes our anger clouds our love. Please help us stay grounded and find understanding. Amen.

When I am having a bad day, and the last thing I want to do is love, I love anyway. This is when God calls upon me the most to get out of my bubble and give comfort to someone else who might need it. In turn, I begin to feel more loving, towards myself, towards others, and towards humanity. God knows that the best way to find the love we seek is to give it.

Behold, what manner of love the Father hath bestowed upon us, that we should be called the sons of God: therefore the world knoweth us not, because it knew him not.

1 John 3:1

If only we could possibly know just how much we are loved, by each other, and by God. We would then know that miracles truly exist and all things are possible. Love gives us wings. Tell someone you love them today.

Lord, dismiss us with thy blessing,
Hope, and comfort from above;
Let us each, thy peace possessing,
Triumph in redeeming love.

—Robert Hawker

God, make me an open vessel through which the waters of your Spirit flow freely. Let your love move through me and out into my world, touching everyone I come in contact with. Express your joy through the special talents you have given me, that others may come to know your presence in their own lives by witnessing your presence in mine. Amen.

God! Thou art love! I build my faith
on that...
I know thee, who hast kept my path,
and made
Light for me in darkness, tempering sorrow
So that it reached me like a solemn joy;
It were too strange that I should doubt
thy love.

—Robert Browning, "Paracelsus"

Count neither the hours nor the seconds
That filled your mind with doubts and fears.
Do not add up unhappy moments,
When pain and hardships brought you to tears.
Regard not days on faded calendars
That marked the passage of your years.
Instead, count heaven's blessings...
Grandchildren playing on the floor,
Old friends walking through the door,
White clouds drifting up above,
And, like a faithful timepiece, God's love.

I will sing unto the Lord, because he hath dealt bountifully with me.

Psalm 13:6

If I count the things I've asked for that you have not given me, I begin to believe you do not love me, God. But if, instead, I bring to mind all of the goodness you have shown me, I come to trust that you have never given me less than what I need and often have blessed me with far more from a depth of love I cannot comprehend.

Let thy mercy, O Lord, be upon us, according as we hope in thee.

Psalm 33:22

Lord, we want to live life to its fullest. And although we know we shouldn't place our own wants before others' wants, it is so easy to think our dreams for the future matter most. Remind us to make compromises. Our love can get us further in this life than selfishness. Amen.

When joy and laughter vanish
Into illness and despair,
I remind myself that with God's help
You can get there from here.
So let not doubt and fear take seed
And grow into a tree,
But let God's healing make me whole
And love take root in me.

As the Father hath loved me, so have I loved you: continue ye in my love.

If ye keep my commandments, ye shall abide in my love; even as I have kept my Father's commandments, and abide in his love.

John 15:9–10

Love. It seems so simple. Love is a gift given. Yet, if we don't overlook it, Lord, we treat it like a gift certificate saved so long it expires. We are down-on-our-knees grateful your gifts of love and grace never expire. Nudge us to use them, for we lose their value each day they go unclaimed. We stay disconnected from you, the source of creation and re-creation. To connect only requires a "Yes!" from us. Hear us shout!

A new commandment I give unto you,
That ye love one another; as I have loved you, that ye also love one another.

By this shall all men know that ye are my disciples, if ye have love one to another.

John 13:34–35

Father, unity among your people is precious to you—and precious to us as well. We cannot achieve it without your assistance, though. Help us to keep petty disagreements from dividing us. Give us the grace to work through any disagreement with love and understanding.

*With all lowliness and meekness,
with longsuffering, forbearing one
another in love;
Endeavouring to keep the unity of the
Spirit in the bond of peace.*

Ephesians 4:2–3

Father, help us to touch and influence others. We want them to recognize and celebrate even the small blessings. We want to surprise them with gestures of love. Amen.

As we learn to trust you, God, we discover your strengthening presence in various places and people. Wherever we encounter shelter, comfort, rest, and peace, we are bound to hear your voice, welcoming us. And in whomever we find truth, love, gentleness, and humility, we are sure to hear your heartbeat, assuring us that you will always be near. Thank you, God. Amen.

Heavenly Father, you are the author of love. We are able to love only because you first loved us. You taught us how to love you and each other—our family and our neighbors. We want everyone to know your perfect love, and we invite the fragrance of your love to permeate our home.

But as it is written, Eye hath not seen, nor ear heard, neither have entered into the heart of man, the things which God hath prepared for them that love him.

1 Corinthians 2:9

Father, nothing moves me more to love others than reflecting on how you love me. I think of all the things you could have held against me and used as reasons to not love me. And yet you always look for ways to forgive, restore our relationship, and move forward.

Thy mercy, O Lord, is in the heavens; and thy faithfulness reacheth unto the clouds.

Thy righteousness is like the great mountains; thy judgments are a great deep: O Lord, thou preservest man and beast.

How excellent is thy lovingkindness, O God! therefore the children of men put their trust under the shadow of thy wings.

Psalm 36:5–7

I know yours is a persistent devotion, Lord. Your devoted love for me is the example that helps me to love others as well. What would I prefer to your love? What could I love more than those I hold dear? Nothing in the universe! Who are the loves of my life? Let me count them all and delight in them today.

Father, when I don't have another ounce of strength to give, you give me gallons of love to fuel my spirit. When I think I can't continue, you push me further and steady my steps. Thank you, God.

Where God is, our comfort and hope is. The divine presence blesses us when we walk in his light and do his will. We are bearers of light and love to all those we meet. We are his divinely inspired earthbound angels.

Lift up thine eyes to see the light
that heals the sick and makes wrongs right.
Lift up thine heart to feel the love
that emanates from God above.

Heavenly Father, it is good to remember that everything that lives and breathes is sacred to you. We must never feel superior to any other human being—for we are all precious in your eyes. You have given us life, and we must make the choices that lead to kindness and peace. You created us, but how we live together is up to us. Thank you.

There is no fear in love; but perfect love casteth out fear: because fear hath torment. He that feareth is not made perfect in love.

1 John 4:18

I know you will not fail to lift me up from my sorrow and gently deposit me upon the shore. And though my body is tired and my spirit is weary from weeping, I offer myself to you in complete surrender, so that you may fill my nets with the bounty of your eternal peace and the comfort of your infinite love.

O Lord, your gift of love is often distorted in this world of ours. You are the source of the only perfect love we will ever know. Thank you, Lord, for abiding in us and helping us love ourselves and others. On this day, Lord, I pray that you will draw near to anyone who is feeling unloved. May they accept your unconditional love so they will know what true love is!

Greater love hath no man than this, that a man lay down his life for his friends.

John 15:13

Lord, I know I encounter them every day: your loved ones who are—on their own strength—desperately trying to make some sense out of this life. Help me reach out to them. Give me the words to say and the gentle approach that will lead them to the knowledge of you and to the immense blessings you want to bestow on them.

I know that when I am sad, lonely, and afraid, I can turn to God for his loving grace. With mercy and compassion, God hears my cries and comes to my aid, ready to take away my burdens and heal my wounded heart. He gives me wisdom and understanding, and helps me to forgive those who have hurt me. God's unceasing love for me is what grace is all about.

How good it is, Almighty One, to bask in the warmth of your love. To know that all that is required of me is this: to receive your good gifts from above.

Though I walk in the midst of trouble, thou wilt revive me: thou shalt stretch forth thine hand against the wrath of mine enemies, and thy right hand shall save me.

The Lord will perfect that which concerneth me: thy mercy, O Lord, endureth for ever: forsake not the works of thine own hands.

Psalm 138:7–8

Lord, your word created all there is. Let it now create a powerful restoration within me. Your love sustains all life. Let it now sustain and renew me. Your strength holds up the galaxies. Let it now hold me up and give me support. Your light reaches the far ends of the universe. Let it shine its healing energy upon me now. Amen.

Save me, O God; for the waters are come in unto my soul. I sink in deep mire, where there is no standing: I am come into deep waters, where the floods overflow me. I am weary of my crying: my throat is dried: mine eyes fail while I wait for my God.

Psalm 69:1–3

The Lord thy God in the midst of thee is mighty; he will save, he will rejoice over thee with joy; he will rest in his love, he will joy over thee with singing.

Zephaniah 3:17

Encircle me in the arms of your love.
Fill me with your perfect peace.
Though my soul faints,
Sustain me through hope in your word.

From the dark night of the soul
Comes the blessing of the dawn.
From the deep wounds of the heart
Comes the gift of love reborn.
From the chaos of confusion
Comes the calm of clarity.
From the anguish of discord
Comes the peace of harmony.
From the grieving of great loss
Comes the happiness of new life.
From the coldness of despair
Comes the warmth of our Father's light.

Chapter 2

Forgiveness

And be ye kind one to another, tenderhearted, forgiving one another, even as God for Christ's sake hath forgiven you.

Ephesians 4:32

And when ye stand praying, forgive, if ye have ought against any: that your Father also which is in heaven may forgive you your trespasses.

Mark 11:25

Father, I need to understand that forgiveness is not dependent on my feelings but rather on a determination of my will. Help me form a few well-chosen words of forgiveness. Amen.

Forgiveness is the central virtue in God's treasure chest—God's forgiveness of us and our forgiveness of others and ourselves. At times we find that forgiveness comes very easily, even for grievous and painful hurts. But many times, we seem powerless to forgive, no matter how hard we try. This is when God's forgiving grace has the opportunity to touch and change us and then be extended to others through our example.

Say not thou,
I will recompense evil;
but wait on the Lord, and he
shall save thee.

Proverbs 20:22

God, I pray for the strength and the wisdom to know what to do in this situation. I pray for enough love to forgive this person for the pain they have caused me and to forgive myself for the ill will I have harbored against this person. Help me be a truly forgiving person so that the weight of resentment may be lifted from my shoulders. Amen.

And when they were come to the place, which is called Calvary, there they crucified him, and the malefactors, one on the right hand, and the other on the left.

Then said Jesus, Father, forgive them; for they know not what they do. And they parted his raiment, and cast lots.

Luke 23:33–34

Heavenly Father, I ask for your healing presence. Protect me from the worldly hurts and evil that have clouded my life and robbed me of joy. Help me forget the past, to let go of grudges, and to make a new start. Take away the darkness of my sorrow, and flood it with the light of your love. Forgive me, so I might forgive others. Amen.

Lord, you have seen each time when I've been abandoned by those in whose love I have trusted. You have known the loneliness in my soul. I must confess to you that it causes me to wonder if your love has failed me, too. I need you to assure me that you are still here and that you will always stay with me.

Heavenly Father, teach me to forgive others their transgressions and to let go of angers and resentments that poison the heart and burden the soul. Teach me to love and understand others and to accept them as they are, not as I wish they would be. Amen.

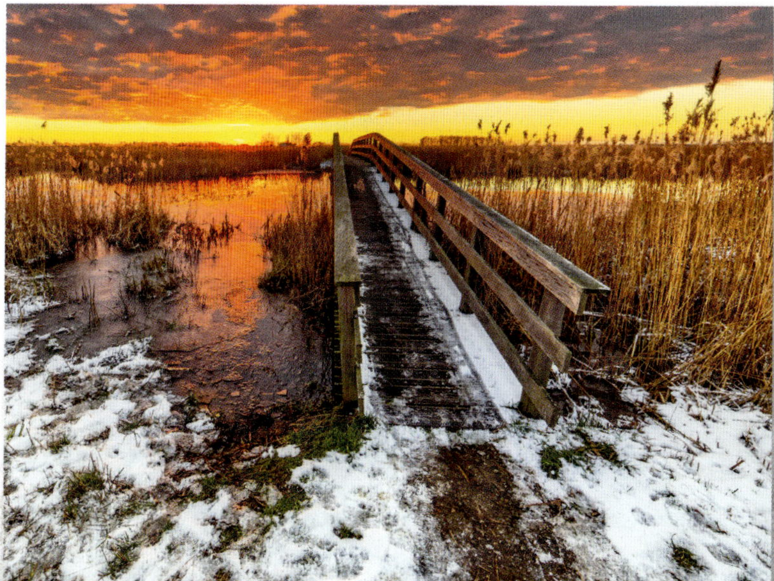

For he shall have judgment without mercy, that hath shewed no mercy; and mercy rejoiceth against judgment.

James 2:13

Dear God, the wound between this person and me seems too deep to heal, and the chasm of misunderstanding seems to wide to leap across. I pray for guidance that I may do my part to close the wound and narrow the gap between us with love, understanding and forgiveness. Amen.

So that contrariwise ye ought rather to forgive him, and comfort him, lest perhaps such a one should be swallowed up with overmuch sorrow.

2 Corinthians 2:7

Father, when we stand to cross the metaphorical bridge of forgiveness, please give us a little push to get us going. Amen.

Judge not, and ye shall not be judged: condemn not, and ye shall not be condemned: forgive, and ye shall be forgiven.

Luke 6:37

Lord, I need you to help me with the concept of forgiving people over and over again for the same behavior. I know you taught that there was no limit to the number of times we should forgive someone, but I get so weary of doing it, Lord. Help me to have a heart of forgiveness, so ready to forgive that I do so before the person who has wronged me even seeks my forgiveness. There's freedom in that kind of forgiveness, Lord. Help me claim it for my own. Amen.

Comfort me in my day of need with a love that is infinite and true. Ignore my lack of desire to forgive and forget. Fill my anger with the waters of peace and serenity that I may come to accept this situation and move on to a greater level of understanding and knowing.

Finally, be ye all of one mind, having compassion one of another, love as brethren, be pitiful, be courteous:

Not rendering evil for evil, or railing for railing: but contrariwise blessing; knowing that ye are thereunto called, that ye should inherit a blessing.

1 Peter 3:8–9

God, I do not intend to hurt you and others. I am not always sure what happens in those times when I do hurt you and others. I am thankful that you forgive. Please help others to forgive me, too. Remind us all to follow your teachings. We pray that you will guide and comfort us.

Lord, what comfort I find in the knowledge that you know everything I've ever done. I know going over my sins with you is still necessary for my growth and development, but it helps to know I'll never have to hear you say, "I can't believe you did that!" You know my strengths and my weaknesses. You know my joy and my shame. And yet you still forgive me and have hope for me. Thank you, Lord, for caring enough to truly know me—and for loving me anyway.

Heavenly Father, give us the forgiving spirit we so badly need to heal the wounds of the past. Help us live "the better life" by making peace with our enemies and understanding that they, too, need your love. Amen.

And all things are of God, who hath reconciled us to himself by Jesus Christ, and hath given to us the ministry of reconciliation;

To wit, that God was in Christ, reconciling the world unto himself, not imputing their trespasses unto them; and hath committed unto us the word of reconciliation.

2 Corinthians 5:18–19

I pray, Lord, for the ability to learn forgiveness. Often within my heart there is much that is negative. I pray to learn to let go of those feelings. I pray to learn to forgive others as I wish to be forgiven. I pray for the gifts of understanding and compassion as I strive to be more like you. Amen.

Then came Peter to him, and said, Lord, how oft shall my brother sin against me, and I forgive him? till seven times?

Jesus saith unto him, I say not unto thee, Until seven times: but, Until seventy times seven.

Matthew 18:21–22

Father God, we know that to receive the blessing of healing, the heart must be open. But when we are mad, we close off the heart as if it were a prison. Remind us that a heart that is shut cannot receive understanding, acceptance, and renewal. Even though we feel angry, we must keep the heart's door slightly ajar so your grace can enter and fill our darkness with the light of hope.

If my people, which are called by my name, shall humble themselves, and pray, and seek my face, and turn from their wicked ways; then will I hear from heaven, and will forgive their sin, and will heal their land.

2 Chronicles 7:14

Lord, it is tempting and easy to cast a scornful eye on those around us and note every fault. When my pride tempts me to do so, prompt me to turn the magnifying glass on myself instead. If I keep in mind how much I need your forgiveness every day, my love for you will never grow cold. I know you are willing to forgive each and every fault if I only ask.

Lord, I confess to you,
sadly, my sin;
all I am, I tell to you,
all I have been.
Purge all my sin away,
wash clean my soul
this day;
Lord, make me clean.
Then all is peace and
light this soul within;
thus shall I walk with you,
loved though unseen.
Leaning on you, my God,
guided along the road,
nothing between!

—Horatius Bonar

Dear God,

Help my unbelief.

When I'm in pain, I forget that
you care about me.

I forget that you have helped me
through my trials.

I forget that you hold me in your arms to keep
me safe.

I forget that you are feeling my pain with me.

I forget that you love me,

I forget that I am important to you.

Show me your presence—let me feel your
enveloping love.

Heal my hurting soul.

Thank you for staying with me even in my unbelief.

Amen.

When will the rain let up, Lord?
Oh, soon: may your presence be to me
as cleansing droplets of mercy, these
clouds only filtering in glorious gold and
purple the blazing rays of your grace.

Lord, why is it that frustration sometimes turns to despair and self-destruction? There are so many destructive forces in the world as it is, why do I sometimes make a bad situation worse because of my bitter or hopeless attitude? How often I wish I could take back thoughtless, hurtful words I have said to a loved one during the course of a trying day. How many times I wish I could have a "do over." But there are no "do overs" in real life. Help me to make amends and handle things better the next time I am challenged.

Forgive us, Lord, our sins, for failing to live up to your standards of goodness and justice. We confess our shortcomings. Make us willing to change and help us become persons of godly character. Amen.

Deliver me, O God, from a
slothful mind,
from all lukewarmness, and all
dejection of spirit. I know these
cannot but deaden my love to
you; mercifully free my heart
from them, and give me a lively,
zealous, active, and cheerful
spirit, that I may vigorously
perform whatever you command,
thankfully suffer whatever you
choose for me, and be ever ardent
to obey in all things your holy love.

—John Wesley

Even if we feel we've been wronged by someone, if we soften our hearts and forgive the one who wronged us, the burden of bitterness will be lifted. This change is certain to affect the lives of those around us.

Whatever the relationship, forgiveness is a truly healing gift for the people involved. In a marriage, the power of true forgiveness cannot be overstated.

When we learn to forgive the past, we sow the seeds for a glorious future.

Even though we may call ourselves "loving," often we justify an action by saying, "he deserved that." When someone comes against us with evil and we respond with good, we are showing mercy.

For if ye forgive men
their trespasses,
your heavenly Father will also
forgive you:

But if ye forgive not men their
trespasses, neither will your
Father forgive your trespasses.

Matthew 6:14–15

God knows that as hard as we may try, there are times when we will make human mistakes. Even so, if we trust in him and ask his forgiveness, he will bless us with mercy and peace.

First we are hurt, and feelings of anger may consume us. Then thoughts of how we can get revenge come creeping in. But only when we are ready to relinquish the hurt is there an opportunity for forgiveness and healing to begin.

Forgiveness is not easy. Often it requires us to become far more than we were before; more mature, more accepting, and more compassionate. But once we forgive and stretch ourselves, we can never go back to being that unforgiving and resentful person we were before. We have been opened up, expanded, and set free.

And they shall teach no more every man his neighbour, and every man his brother, saying, Know the Lord: for they shall all know me, from the least of them unto the greatest of them, saith the Lord: for I will forgive their iniquity, and I will remember their sin no more.

Jeremiah 31:34

God prefers that we make an effort, even if we should initially fail. He will eagerly forgive our mistakes in the hope that we will learn and grow from them.

Let your anger set with the sun and not rise again with it.

—Irish Proverb

One of the greatest peace-robbers in our lives is anger. It affects our minds, our bodies, and our emotions. If we choose to let go of it, we can embrace peace again.

God pardons like a mother who kisses the offense into everlasting forgetfulness.

—Henry Ward Beecher

Chapter 3

Nature

I will speak of the glorious honour of thy majesty, and of thy wondrous works.

Psalm 145:5

Lord, I can hear your voice in the bubbling brook, see your beauty in the petals of a flower, and feel your gentle breath in the evening breeze and in the soft kiss of a child. Thank you for all of these gifts.

Although the rain still falls, Creator God, it takes such a little bit of sun to create a rainbow, your sign of promise and presence.

Holy Spirit, the life that gives life.
You are the cause of all movement;
You are the breath of all creatures;
You are the salve that purifies
our souls;
You are the ointment that heals
our wounds;
You are the fire that warms
our hearts;
You are the light that guides our feet.
Let all the world praise you.

—Hildegard of Bingen

The heavens are thine, the earth also is thine: as for the world and the fulness thereof, thou hast founded them.

Psalm 89:11

It's easy to praise you for your majesty and power when we see thundering waterfalls, crashing ocean waves, or majestic sunsets. Help us learn to praise you when we see a dewdrop, a seedling, or an ant.

I am grateful, God of Hope, for the gift of each new day, each new season, like the one unfolding around me now in flower and birdsong, in seedling and bud. When they arrive as surely as dawn follows night and bloom follows bulb, I am uplifted by the fulfillment of your promise.

Little drops of water,
Little grains of sand,
Make the mighty ocean
And the pleasant land.
Little deeds of kindness,
Little words of love,
Help to make earth happy
Like the heaven above.

—Julia Fletcher Carney

I have made the earth, the man and the beast that are upon the ground, by my great power and by my outstretched arm, and have given it unto whom it seemed meet unto me.

Jeremiah 27:5

And God called the dry land Earth; and the gathering together of the waters called he Seas: and God saw that it was good.

Genesis 1:10

Like sun that melts the snow,
my soul absorbs the grace
that beats in gentle, healing rays
from some godly place.
Like rain that heals parched earth,
my body drinks the love
that falls in gently, soothing waves
from heaven up above.

God, I couldn't help noticing all the loveliness you placed in the world today! This morning I witnessed a sunrise that made my heart beat faster. Then, later, I watched a father gently help his child across a busy parking lot; his tenderness was much like yours. While inside a department store, I spied an elderly couple sitting on a bench. I could hear the man cracking jokes; their laughter lifted my spirits. Then early this evening, I walked by a woman tending her flower bed; she took great pleasure in her work, and her garden was breathtaking. Later, I talked with a friend who is helping some needy families; her genuine compassion inspired me. Thank you, Lord, for everything that is beautiful and good in the world.

Father, make me resilient like the sandy beach upon which the waves crash. Make me strong like the mighty willow tree that bends but does not break in the high winds. Give me the patience and wisdom to know that my suffering will one day turn to a greater understanding of your ways, your works, and your wonders.

God, you are so great. It is always the right time to worship you, but morning is best. Praise for the dawning light that streams in through this window. Praise for the sound of the birds as they flit through in the air. Praise for the little spider crawling along on the ceiling. Praise for the smell of coffee and the warmth of a cup in my hands. Praise for the flowering plants—and even those weeds growing by the house. Praise for the neighbors walking along the sidewalk and the clouds moving by, too. Most of all, praise for the breath that keeps flowing in and out of my lungs. Yes, this is the greatest item of praise: that you alone are my life—all life itself. Without you, all is dust. Praise . . . for you.

We thank thee,
O Lord whose finger touched our dust,
O Lord who gave us breath.
We thank thee, Lord, who gave us sight and sense
to see the flower,
to hear the wind,
to feel the waters in our hand,
to sleep with the night and wake with the sun,
to stand upon this star,
to sing thy praise,
to hear thy voice.

Lord, it's so easy for us to get bogged down in the details of life on this earth. But when we have the opportunity to gaze up at the stars on a clear night, it is easy to remember that there is so much more to your creation than our relatively insignificant lives. You placed the stars and know them by name, Lord, and you know us by name too. We are blessed to be even a tiny part of your magnificent creation! That you also care so deeply for us is the best gift of all.

Bless the soil beneath our feet, the sky overhead, and make us one with it. We are catching on, catching up with ourselves, creator God, and catching a whiff of the garbage we're burying ourselves beneath. Catching, too, a glimpse of the fading streams and trash-strewn seas we have long ignored.

Bless and use our reclamation efforts, for it is a task we can't accomplish alone. With your help, we can bind up and reclaim this poor old earth. We feel whispers of hope in the winds of changed hearts and minds, for we recall your promise to make all things new—even this earth we shall yet learn to tend. We are grateful for another chance.

Deep peace of the running waves to you.
Deep peace of the flowing air to you.
Deep peace of the smiling stars to you.
Deep peace of the quiet earth to you.
Deep peace of the watching shepherds
to you.
Deep peace of the Son of Peace to you.

—Gaelic Prayer

We are blessed by your enveloping spirit as near to us as daily changing weather. Your comfort touches us like the gentle rain and the hushed snow. And, like the sound of thunder and glimpse of searing lightning, you startle us with new opportunities.

Winters can be long, Lord, as I've complained before, and hope elusive. Thank you for sending me outdoors. My spirit soars at the sight of a woodchuck waking from winter sleep. I rub sleep from my eyes, grateful for signposts of change, like pawprints in the mud, leading me to springs of the soul.

Creation shouts to me, Lord, about how amazing you are. I see the wonder of your wisdom in everything from the solar system to how bodies of water feed into one another to the life cycles of all living creatures. Everywhere I turn there is something that makes me think about how creative and insightful you are. Thank you for this universe that speaks without words. I hear it loud and clear, and it tells me of your magnificence.

Lord, we praise you for all the beauty and wonder you've placed in the world. How creative of you to think of a creature as exuberant and joyful as the hummingbird! How interesting that you sprinkled spots on the backs of the newborn fawns that follow along behind their mother through our backyard. Let us never become so accustomed to your glorious creation that we take it for granted, Lord. You've blessed us with a wonderland, and we thank you for it.

Blessings often come to us shaded
in disguise.
Miracles work magic veiled from human eyes.
Knowing healing comes from pain,
that every loss makes way for gain,
or that the sun shines after rain,
and what goes round comes back again,
marks the difference between the ignorant and
the wise.

Like the weather, love has its change of seasons. It begins with the springtime of courtship, merging into the sweet summer of devotion. When autumn arrives, so, too, do the rewards of commitment and sharing. Winter often brings a sense of comfort and contentment, but just as the weather is cyclical, so, too, is love. Just beyond winter is an even brighter spring of renewed passion, internal beauty, and deeper devotion.

Hope melts the frost from the tiniest leaf, allowing it to grow stronger in the healing light of the sun.

Living in harmony with nature's seasons awakens us to spring's renewal, fall's cozy slowness, winter's savory rest, and summer's exuberance. Thus we are reminded to honor each season's energies for the wisdom they hold.

Faith is like a tiny seed of belief inside us that grows into a mighty tree, each leaf a new direction, each branch a new opportunity.

Enjoy all of creation, each leaf and flower and every small pebble along the way. Embrace the hope of each new morning, and the last ray of sunshine to fall at day's end.

Beautiful pastel colors,
Pink, blue, golden, white,
Brightening every highway and byway,
Colors soft and light.
Covering the earth in a rosy glow,
A special sunset for all to see.
Brushstrokes of heavenly beauty
On a canvas that spans the seas.
I can't describe my feelings
As I watch him paint the sky,
A sense of solace covers the earth
As another day goes by.

Like the evergreen, hope never dies, but stands tall and mighty against the coldest winter winds until the summer sun returns to warm its outstretched branches.

When we struggle in the search for harmony, we need only remember to look for nature for the answer.

In the solitude of a natural setting, the heart discovers serenity, the soul knows abiding peace, and the spirit finds renewal.

The world acquired a new interest when birds appeared, for the presence of birds at any time is magical in effect. They are magicians that transform every scene; make of every desert a garden of delights.

—Charles C. Abbott

In the peaceful quiet of a dark night, the moon's beauty catches your eye and captures your soul.

Seated on an outcropping of rock high above the snowbound valley, my eye is drawn to the evergreen, and hope stirs within my breast.

The heart of the mountain is the wild ravine where these two streams mingle in coolness and shadow. No path leads to it and few are the feet which have found a way to its beauty. There is a peculiar charm in a spot unknown to the many. Its loneliness endears it to the mind, and gives its associations a rarer flavor.

—Frank Bolles

Kindness sows a seed within me that begins to sprout where before all was barren. Leaves of trust start to bud, and I branch out. I take in gentle caring and loving nudging and realize I might just go ahead and bloom! After all, God arranged spring after winter.

Chapter 4

Giving Thanks

In every thing give thanks: for this is the will of God in Christ Jesus concerning you.

1 Thessalonians 5:18

Thank you, God, that even when I fret, I know without a doubt that you are using my unique, special gifts and talents to nurture and teach my children. When I get down on myself and am unsure of my abilities, remind me that your commitment to me is lifelong.

God, I give thanks for the wisdom you share with me when I am trying to understand my own actions or someone else's. You know what is best, and you have my highest good in mind. I will turn to you for the advice and guidance I need. Thank you, God, for being a strong and loving presence in my life. Amen.

Lord, you are the light I follow down this long, dark tunnel. You are the voice that whispers, urging me onward when this wall of sorrow seems insurmountable. You are the hand that reaches out and grabs mine when I feel as if I'm sinking in despair. You alone, Lord, are the waters that fill me when I am dried of all hope and faith. I thank you, Lord, for although I may feel like giving up, you have not given up on me. Amen.

And when ye will offer a sacrifice
of thanksgiving unto the Lord,
offer it at your own will.

Leviticus 22:29

God, we thank you for this food
for the hands that planted it
for the hands that tended it
for the hands that harvested it
for the hands that preprared it
for the hands that provided it
and for the hands that served it.
And we pray for those without
enough food
in your world and in our land of plenty.

O Lord, we give thanks for your presence, which greets us each day in the guise of a friend, a work of nature, or a stranger's story. We are reminded through these messengers in our times of need that you are indeed watching over us. Lord, we have known you in the love and care of a friend, who envelops and keeps us company in our despair. When we observe the last morning glory stretching faithfully to receive what warmth is left in the chilly sunshine, we are heartened and inspired to do the same. When we are hesitant to speak up and then read in the newspaper a story of courage and controversy, we find our voice lifted and strengthened by your message in plain type. Lord, we are grateful receivers of all the messages that surround us every day.

Give thanks unto the Lord, call upon his name, make known his deeds among the people.

1 Chronicles 16:8

Gracious and healing God, thank you for everything you have done for me in the past.

You have restored me in unexpected ways and I will never be the same.

Thank you for being with me in the present and for the bright future you have planned for me. I pray for those who don't know you yet, who don't understand how you bless them again and again.

Use me to share the gratitude I feel, that others may grow to know you and your power.

In the name of Jesus, who healed the sick and made the lame to walk, I pray. Amen.

Lord, help my eyes to see all the ways you are working in this world. Because of your great compassion, because of your active involvement, the effects of everything you accomplish are multiplied many times over. We praise you, Lord, and pray you will continue to be involved in our lives and in our world. And may our deeds and thoughts always honor you.

No matter
the worries I have,
small or large,
you, O God, are
there ahead of me
with promises of
help and support
that relieve me
and free me from
getting stuck in
the mire of my
fear. I am grateful.

O Lord, please help me to understand that I won't always get what I pray for. In the same regard, I want to learn to thank you more for everything you do give me. Amen.

For the promise you unfold with the opening of each day, I thank you, Lord.

For blessings shared along the way, I thank you, Lord.

For the comfort of our home filled with love to keep us warm, I thank you, Lord.

For shelter from the winter storm, I thank you, Lord.

For the gifts of peace and grace you grant the family snug within, I thank you, Lord.

For shielding us from harm and sin, I thank you, Lord.

For the beauty of the snow sparkling in the winter sun, I thank you, Lord.

For the peace when the day is done, I thank you, Lord.

Dear Lord, when I am sad, you give me hope. When I am lost, you offer me direction and guidance. When I am alone, you stand beside me. When my heart aches with sorrow, you bring me new blessings. Thank you for your gifts of grace, of love, and of healing. Amen.

God, help me notice the little things and be grateful for them. All too often, we rush through life and don't notice the blessings all around us. I am grateful for the chance to see beauty in the smallest details. Help me remember to slow down and look. I am grateful for the little bits of beauty scattered through my day.

To the end that my glory may sing praise to thee, and not be silent. O Lord my God, I will give thanks unto thee forever.

Psalm 30:12

Lord, if I were to boil down all the good news in the universe and look to see what I'd ended up with, there would be the eternal realities of your goodness, your love, and your faithfulness. And in this world, I don't have to look far for them—family, food, shelter, clothing, seasons, tides, sun, moon, stars, life, beauty, truth, salvation. And that's just a sampling, a preview of a much longer list. I'm moved to praise you and to tell you how much I love you back.

Lord, we stand in awe of your great sacrifice for us. Your journey to the cross is the reason we are free from the destruction of sin. It's why we can be forgiven and be united with you throughout eternity. No sacrifice is too great in response to your love for us. Keep us ever mindful, Lord. Keep us ever grateful.

I will give thee thanks in the great congregation: I will praise thee among much people.

Psalm 35:18

Dear Lord, thank you for healing my heart and bringing joy and meaning back into my life. Thank you for the people who truly care for me. Help me be a soothing and joyful presence in their lives as well. Amen.

Thank you for your wise ways, Lord. Following them fills my life with true blessings—the riches of love and relationship, joy and provision, peace and protection. I remember reading in your Word that whenever I ask for your wisdom from a faith-filled heart, you will give it, no holds barred. So I'll ask once again today for your insight and understanding as I build, using your blueprints.

I will praise the name of God with a song, and will magnify him with thanksgiving.

Psalm 69:30

We praise you, Lord, for eternal life. And we thank you for your love for each one of us. Amen.

There's so much to be grateful for in this life! Thank you, God, for your many blessings.

Savior, like a shepherd lead us,
Much we need thy tender care;
In thy pleasant pastures feed us,
For our use thy folds prepare.
Blessed Jesus, blessed Jesus,
Thou hast bought us, thine we are.
Blessed Jesus, blessed Jesus,
Thou hast bought us, thine we are.

—Dorothy A. Thrupp

Wondrous God, I praise your name.
Your Word is life.
I believe you can heal me.
Be with me when I am sick, and remind me
to praise you when I am well.
Thank you for healing me in the past,
And for future healing.
Keep me in good health
That I might serve you
And praise your name.
Amen.

We plow the fields and scatter
The good seed on the land,
But it is fed and watered
By God's almighty hand;
He sends the snow in winter,
The warmth to swell the grain,
The breezes and the sunshine,
And soft, refreshing rain.
All good gifts around us
Are sent from heaven above:
Then thank the Lord,
O thank the Lord
For all His love.

—Matthias Claudius

And he took the cup, and gave thanks, and gave it to them, saying, Drink ye all of it.

Matthew 26:27

Gratitude is an attitude of loving what you have, and this undoubtedly leads to having even more. When you open your eyes to the bountiful blessings already in your life, you realize just how abundant the world really is. Suddenly, you feel more giving, more loving, and more open to even greater blessings. Gratitude is a key that unlocks the door to treasures you already have, and it yields greater treasures yet to be discovered.

Gratitude may be the most underestimated of virtues. We think of love, hope, faith, and the power of prayer and forgiveness. But how often do we stop each day and give thanks for all the blessings in our lives? Are we too focused on what we lack, what we don't have, don't want, don't need? By opening the heart and mind to focus on gratitude, we unleash a treasure of unceasing good that's just waiting to overflow into our lives. A grateful person knows that by giving thanks, they're given even more to be thankful for.

Thank you, God, for second chances. Sometimes I feel like I can't do anything right. It's embarrassing to make mistakes. It's embarrassing to show others that I am less than perfect. Thank you for giving me the chance to try again, to make things right, and to improve myself. Help me find the courage to try again and show the world my best qualities!

Now thank we all our God
with hearts and hands and voices,
who wondrous things hath done,
in whom this world rejoices;
who, from our mothers' arms,
hath blessed us on our way
with countless gifts of love,
and still is ours today.

—Martin Rinkart, translated by
Catherine Winkworth

Thank you, Lord, for reaching out and drawing me under your wings. Even though I am just one of billions of people who need you, your love is so great that you know my troubles, are concerned for my welfare, and are working to renew my dreams. I am so blessed to have you to turn to when I am faced with a calamity, and I am so very grateful that I have you to lean on. I praise you with all my heart. Amen.

Thank God when the pain ends, when once again we're well and whole and strong. Thank God when our bodies are released from the blinding, mind-numbing hurts that affect our whole lives. Thank God when we have complete victory over pain.

The most important prayer in the world is just two words long: "Thank You."

—Meister Eckhart

Water that runs over moss-covered rocks: This is the sound of praise. Fingers that play upon ivory keys: This is the sound of worship. Silence that speaks even better than words: This is the sound of my thankful heart.

*Blessed and praised be the Lord,
from whom comes all the good that
we speak and think and do.*

—Teresa of Avila

Gratitude lifts us, like angels, above the cares that weigh us to the earth.

Cherish the chance to work and play and think and speak and sing; all simple pleasures are opportunities for grateful praise.

When did you last pause to recognize God's wisdom in the timing of events in your life? Have you thanked Him?

O worship the King, all glorious above, O gratefully sing His power and His love.

—Robert Grant

Chapter 5

Joy

And all the people came up after him, and the people piped with pipes, and rejoiced with great joy, so that the earth rent with the sound of them.

1 Kings 1:40

In his neck remaineth strength, and sorrow is turned into joy before him.

Job 41:22

God, grant me the courage to let go of shame, guilt, and anger. Free me of all negative energies, for only then will I become a conduit for joy and a channel for goodness. Amen.

Take time to work—
It is the price of success.
Take time to think—
It is the source of power.
Take time to play—
It is the secret of perpetual youth.
Take time to read—
It is the fountain of wisdom.
Take time to be friendly—
It is the road to happiness.
Take time to dream—
It is hitching your wagon to a star.
Take time to love and be loved—
It is the privilege of the gods.
Take time to look around—
It is too short a day to be selfish.
Take time to laugh—
It is music to the soul.

—Anonymous

Father, this morning I woke up, and the gift of life was still within me. What a privilege! I don't want to lose wonder of it for even one day. So help me to live with purpose and joy, not waiting for what today might bring me, but rather looking for opportunities to be and do all that you've created me for. And, most of all, thank you for being with me in each moment, showing me the way of abundant living.

Thou wilt shew me the path of life: in thy presence is fullness of joy; at thy right hand there are pleasures for evermore.

Psalm 16:11

God, shine your healing light down upon me today, for my path is filled with painful obstacles and my suffering fogs my vision. Clear the challenges from the road I must walk upon, or at least walk with me as I confront them. With you, I know I can endure anything. With you, I know I can make it through to the other side, where joy awaits. Amen.

When we think of joy, we often think of things that are new—a new day, a new baby, a new love, a new beginning, the promise of a new home with God in heaven. Rejoicing in these things originates with having joy in the God who makes all things new. Rather than relying on earthly pleasures to provide happiness, the scriptures command that we rejoice in God and in each new day he brings. Joy is a celebration of the heart that goes beyond circumstances to the very foundation of joy—the knowledge that we are loved by God.

And my soul shall be joyful in the Lord: it shall rejoice in his salvation.

Psalm 35:9

Blessed are you who know how to celebrate the goodness of life. Blessed because you choose to see the grace above and beyond the pain. Blessed because you see a potential friend in every stranger you meet. Blessed because you know the darkest clouds have brilliant silver linings. And most blessed because: All you ever knew of the half-empty glass was that it was almost full.

Whatever is right and pure,
excellent and gracious,
admirable and beautiful,
fill my mind with these things.
Too much of the world
comes to me in tones of gray and brown.
Too great the temptation
to indulge obsessive thoughts and sordid plans.
Guard my mind; place a fence around my motives.
The pure, the lovely, the good—Yes!
Only those today.

God with me lying down,
God with me rising up,
God with me in each ray of light
Nor I a ray of joy without Him,
Nor one ray without Him.

Christ with me sleeping,
Christ with me waking,
Christ with me watching,
Every day and night,
Each day and night.
God with me protecting,
The Lord with me directing,
The Spirit with me
strengthening,
For ever and for evermore,
Ever and evermore,
Amen.

—Celtic Prayer

I wish to extend my love, Lord. So give me hands quick to work on behalf of the weak. Cause my feet to move swiftly in aid of the needy. Let my mouth speak words of encouragement and new life. And give my heart an ever-deepening joy through it all.

Hope is the joyful liberation of the heart from the darkest prison of despair.

Then will I go unto the altar of God, unto God my exceeding joy: yea, upon the harp will I praise thee, O god my God.

Psalm 43:4

Give us eyes with which to see, noses with which to sniff, ears with which to hear the faintest sound along the paths you have set for us, O God of Daily Joys. Following you is a whole experience—body, mind, and soul.

Joy grows in the most unlikely of places. It reaches up in the middle of poverty to dance in the eye of a child at play. It spreads itself across the face of an old man whose rheumatism, while all too present, is forgotten the moment he greets an old friend. Joy wedges itself through the cracks of loneliness when the voice at the other end of the phone line is that of someone familiar and loved. How is it that joy is found where it is least expected? It is, no doubt, because true joy roots itself not in the shifting sands of circumstance but in the rich soil of a grateful heart.

Lord, I do believe! And because of my hope of life with you in eternity, there is all the more meaning for life today. There's meaning in my choices, my relationships, my work, my play, my worship. It all matters, it all counts, and I live knowing one day I'll stand in your presence with great joy.

Cultures throughout the world have used dance to express joy. Dancing is done at feasts, at weddings, and at almost every other celebration. In fact, God's word commands us to dance as an expression of worship and joy.

When we experience true joy, we will naturally express it. As God pours joy into our lives, we can bring this joy to others.

If you truly open your heart
To new opportunities,
You will see
That the possibilities
Are endless.
So look to your future
With the excitement and joy
It truly deserves.

With an eye made quiet by the power of harmony and the deep power of joy, we see into the lives of things.

—William Wordsworth

Angels skip along the seashore picking up shells, kissing each one, and whispering, "Good job!" Angels traipse through the galaxy, touching stars and dancing on planets. Angels waltz through the heavens, full of joy and worship, flowing with majesty, rhythm, and love.

There's a fulfilling joy that comes from serving other people rather than putting our own desires first.

There's a place of renewal and happiness within you. All you need to do to reach it is withdraw your attention from the outside world and focus on the strength and the energy inside yourself.

When I think of God, my heart is so full of joy that the notes leap and dance as they leave my pen: and since God has given me a cheerful heart, I serve him with a cheerful spirit.

—Franz Joseph Haydn

It is wonderful to watch an uninhibited person express joy. We long to give our souls permission to rejoice so freely.

Fill the cup of happiness for others, and there will be enough overflowing to fill yours to the brim.

—Rose Pastor Stokes

Restore unto me the joy of thy salvation; and uphold me with thy free spirit.

Psalm 51:12

How you feel is determined by how you think you feel. If you think you're happy you will be; if you expect good things to happen they will.

To live happily is an inward power of the soul.

—Marcus Aurelius

Sometimes I demand,
"God give me joy!"
and nothing happens.
Yet joy flows naturally,
lavishly, when I seek to
know, love, and
serve him.

There are joys which long to be ours. God sends ten thousand truths, which come about us like birds seeking inlet; but we are shut up to them, and so they bring us nothing, but sit and sing a while upon the roof and then fly away.

—*Henry Ward Beecher,* Life Thoughts

Happiness is contagious! If allowed to spread, it can infect the whole universe with joy.

Make a joyful noise unto the Lord, all the earth: make a loud noise, and rejoice, and sing praise.

Psalm 98:4

Remember, in the first place, that the Vine was the Eastern symbol of Joy. It was its fruit that made glad the heart of man. Yet, however innocent that gladness—for the expressed juice of the grape was the common drink at every peasant's board—the gladness was only a gross and passing thing. This was not true happiness, and the vine of the Palestine vineyards was not the true vine. "Christ was the true Vine." Here, then, is the ultimate source of Joy. Through whatever media it reaches us, all true Joy and Gladness find their source in Christ.

—Henry Drummond

O spread the tidings 'round, wherever man
is found,
wherever human hearts and human woes abound;
let every Christian tongue proclaim the
joyful sound:
The Comforter has come!
The Comforter has come, the Comforter has come!
The Holy Ghost from heaven,
the Father's promise given;
O spread the tidings 'round, wherever man
is found—
the Comforter has come!
The long, long night is past, the morning breaks
at last,
and hushed the dreadful wail and fury of the blast,
as over the golden hills the day advances fast!
The Comforter has come!

—Frank Bottome

They that sow in tears shall reap in joy.

Psalm 126:5

Help us to relax, Lord of calming seas, so that we don't become numb to the joy and awe of children, of family. For it's socially acceptable to kick off our shoes and tangibly feel the love. Make us alive, O God, to the holy grounds of life, and save us from taking these special places for granted.

Today I am thankful for the gift of laughter. How wonderful it is to let out a big belly laugh and feel joy rush through my entire body! Thank you for the people who make me laugh, whether it is a neighbor or friend or a performer on television. Thank you for allowing me to experience joy bursting out of me, and help me make others feel happy with my laughter as well.

We all want to be happy, but joy goes much deeper. Joy is not based on circumstances or feelings, which change like the weather. True joy comes from a celebration of the heart over the things that do not change—things that come from God.

We miss so much joy just because we don't open ourselves up to all there is to enjoy. We can choose to embrace all the joy that today has to bring.

For ye shall go out with joy, and be led forth with peace: the mountains and the hills shall break forth before you into singing, and all the trees in the field shall clap their hands.

Isaiah 55:12

Each sunrise reveals a new opportunity to experience joy.

Mirth is the sweet wine of human life. It should be offered, sparkling with zestful life, unto God.

—Henry Ward Beecher

Chapter 6

Faith

Thy mercy, O Lord, is in the heavens; and thy faithfulness reacheth unto the clouds.

Psalm 36:5

I will sing of the mercies of the Lord for ever: with my mouth will I make known thy faithfulness to all generations.

Psalm 89:1

Lord, perfect for me what is lacking of thy gifts; of faith, help thou mine unbelief; of hope, establish my trembling hope; of love, kindle its smoking flax.

—Lancelot Andrewes

You call me to courage, Lord, but incrementally, as a child emboldened to walk along placing each small foot in larger footprints. Following Father or Mother—as I am following you—knowing a path marked out this way—just step by step—but you can only lead to safety.

Mine eyes shall be upon the faithful of the land, that they may dwell with me: he that walketh in a perfect way, he shall serve me.

Psalm 101:6

I am feeling my way through this darkness, God, and it seems I'm going around in circles. Yet you have just reminded me quietly that I am encircled by your love. With every move I make I go no closer to you—nor farther either—than I already am.

Lord, you are here,
Lord, you are there.
You are wherever we go.
Lord, you guide us,
Lord, you protect us.
You are wherever we go.
Lord, we need you,
Lord, we trust you,
You are wherever we go.
Lord, we love you,
Lord, we praise you,
You are wherever we go.

In silence I kneel in your presence—bow my heart to your wisdom; lift my hands for your mercy. And open my soul to the great gift: I am already held in your arms.

Lord, if we could see the future, it would be easy to have hope. Real hope is when we can't see the end of the road, but still trust you to lead us there.

Thy faithfulness is unto all generations: thou hast established the earth, and it abideth.

Psalm 119:90

Dear Lord, help me to build on a firm foundation by relying on your wisdom, diligently seeking your direction in all I do, learning to walk in your paths of kindness, peace, and justice to my fellow man. In Jesus' name, Amen.

Ah, what solace there is in your promise of peace. True help and real peace are to be found from trusting in your guidance and inspiration.

My trust is in you, God of miracles and surprises, for daily I sense your presence in a dozen ways.

Lord, help me not accuse you of being untrue when I don't get from you everything I want, for you have promised to meet all my needs. And when I learn to love you supremely and trust you wholly, my desires will find fulfillment in you.

O God, giver of all good things, our faith in you is like a treasure to be mined — it sustains, it inspires, and it provides us with unimagined contentment.

Lord, I pray I can find a place within my heart where I can let go of worries. I want to be filled with the calmness of a faith in you. Amen.

When life's winds toss me
upon the waves of uncertainty and doubt,
And when the tempest beats me
and rocks of guilt and self-pity,
When my pitiful heart yearns
for love I cannot find,
When the darkness seems darker
and the night longer,
Some unseen hand reaches down,
and with a strength and tenderness
I cannot comprehend,
Pulls me back into the light.

Lord, open my eyes that I might see
A whole new level of reality.

When I feel surrounded by my problems,

Show me your angelic army surrounding them.

Thank you for the tenacious way they guard me,

Keeping me from potential harm I may never know about.

Let me join my voice with theirs

In praising you, the holy one, the worthy one, the hallelujah victor over all in heaven and earth.

Glory to you in the highest, Lord.

And peace in my little world.

Amen

Lord, you are my lighthouse,
shining like a beacon
in a raging storm,
guiding my way
through the fog and rough seas.

I set my course on you
with patience, perseverance,
and faith, trusting
that you will help me
reach calmer shores.

And when he saw their faith, he said unto him, Man, thy sins are forgiven thee.

Luke 5:20

Dear Heavenly Father, life is full of surprises. Of course, we welcome the good, but when the bad befalls us, we seek reasons for it. It is often in these bad circumstances that we realize how significant and meaningful our faith is. As a result, we pray that you will teach us to always reach out to you. Amen.

Faith is not merely praying
Upon our knees at night;
Faith is not merely straying
Through darkness into light;
Faith is not merely waiting
For glory that may be.
Faith is the brave endeavor,
The splendid enterprise,
The strength to serve, whatever
Conditions may arise.

—Anonymous

Father, there are many events in our lives over which we have no control. However, we do have a choice either to endure trying times or to give up. Remind us that the secret of survival is remembering that our hope is in your fairness, goodness, and justice. When we put our trust in you who cannot fail us, we can remain faithful. Our trust and faithfulness produce the endurance that sees us through the tough times we all face in this life. Please help us to remember. Amen.

And his name through faith in his name hath made this man strong, whom ye see and know: yea, the faith which is by him hath given him this perfect soundness in the presence of you all.

Acts 3:16

Lord, help me to depend on you to be my source of goodness. I don't always feel like being patient, kind, loving, or joyful, but you are all of these things by your very nature. So right now I place my strengths and weaknesses into your hands, asking you to infuse them with yourself and to make them instruments of good that will serve others for your sake.

Dear Father God, you sent your son to us to be our Lord, to watch over us, to bring us comfort, strength, hope, and healing when our hearts are broken and our lives seem shattered. We will never be alone, not when you are here with us always and forever. Remind us to look to you for strength. Amen.

Lord, how it must amuse you at times to see us orchestrating the details of our days as if everything and everyone were in our control. It's only when you are involved in our plans that things go smoothly, Lord. Teach us to trust that your way is the better way, even when we can't see how every detail will turn out. Our insight is only as good as our reliance on you. Please be with us each day, Lord.

Lord, maybe it's in the times we aren't sure that you are hearing our prayers that we learn to trust you the most. Eventually—in your time—we hear your answer. We know that you are still sovereign, and all our hopes and dreams are safe in your hands. Even when the answer to a prayer is "no," we are comforted by the knowledge that you care about us and respond to our concerns in a way that will ultimately be for our good.

Father, scripture makes it clear to me that the life of faith is not passive. While we wait for you to answer prayer, grant wisdom, and open doors, we also keep our minds sharp and our hearts strengthened by reading and studying, by meeting with you in prayer, and by finding encouragement among other believers. These are the disciplines our souls need to stay focused on ever-present hope.

Imagine having someone always beside you to help you navigate the choppy waters of life. Imagine being able to turn within and ask for strength, courage, love, care, or guidance whenever it is needed. The thing is, you do have someone exactly like this, even though you may have forgotten. You have God.

Lord, today I praise you for giving me the faith to believe, for faith itself is a gift from you. I lift up to you today all those I know who are having trouble accepting your gift of salvation. Be patient with them, Lord. Reveal yourself to them in a way that will reach them, and draw them into relationship with you. Our lives are incomplete without you, Lord. Send your grace to those who struggle.

Lord, speak to me, that I may speak
In living echoes of thy tone;
As thou hast sought so let me seek
Thy erring children lost and lone.
O teach me, Lord, that I may teach
The precious things thou dost impart;
And wing my words, that they may reach
The hidden depths of many a heart.
O fill me with thy fullness, Lord,
Until my very heart o'erflow
In kindling thought and glowing word,
Thy love to tell, thy praise to show.

—Frances R. Havergal

God, I hold fast to you at this present moment, for it is the only way for me to have perspective and hope for life beyond this pain I have. And yet, come quickly for I am tired. Fill me with your strength for I feel weak. Add meaning to these days of pain, and finally call me to a new day when I can serve you with a renewed purpose and passion. Amen.

In the midst of mourning life's troubles, you come to us. In the darkness, your spirit moves, spreading light like a shower of stars against a stormy night sky.

Father God, in you I find comfort and peace after a day of working hard and pushing forward to reach my goals. In you I find strength when I've done all I can do on my own. In you I find my spirit renewed. Amen.

If I put my hope in people, I am often disappointed.

If I put my hope in circumstances, I am often let down.

But when I put my hope in God, I am always taken care of.

God is my rock and my hope, in him is a firm foundation from which I live my life. I may not always get all my hoped-for prayers answered the way I expect, but I get them answered the way God wants.

Angels find us, not only when we need them most, but even when we think we are fine on our own.

Time is tight, Lord, and I wonder why I bother to pray. The question is answer enough: I need a relationship where I don't have to bluff and hurry. And when I pray boldly? I offer myself as a possible answer to prayer. No time to waste.

Take comfort in God's steadfast presence.
Even when you suffer, take comfort
in the hope of God's healing.
Even when you fear, take comfort
in the hope of God's strength.
No matter what you face, take comfort
in knowing you never walk alone.

My times are in Thy hand;
My God, I wish them there;
My life, my friends, my soul I leave
Entirely to Thy care.

—William F. Lloyd

Lord, I know you will show your goodness and faithfulness to me if I just diligently seek you. The problem isn't your willingness to give, but my tendency to try to do everything by myself rather than leaning on and trusting in you. This silly inclination brings me needless stress and wastes precious time. Today I endeavor to lay my needs and troubles at your feet the minute I begin to feel the least bit overwhelmed.

*When life seems dark and empty
and there's no hope in sight,
look for God to send an angel
to guide you toward the light.*

Lord, we've tossed our prayers aloft, and hopefully, expectantly, we wait for your answers. As we do, we will: listen, for you speak in the voice of nature; see you as a companion in the face and hand of a friend; feel you as a sweet-smelling rain, a river breeze; believe you can provide encouragement, direction, and guidance for those who have only to ask. We feel your presence.

Chapter 7

Growth

But grow in grace, and in the knowledge of our Lord and Savior Jesus Christ. To him be glory both now and for ever. Amen.

2 Peter 3:18

Change is never easy, but the blessings it bestows upon us are magnificent. Just ask the caterpillar struggling within the tight confines of a cocoon. Even as it struggles, it is becoming something glorious, something beautiful, soon to emerge as a winged butterfly. Change may bring temporary pain and discomfort, but it also brings the promise of a new life filled with joy and freedom and the ability to soar even higher than we ever did before.

Lord, speak to me through these pages.
Let me hear your gentle words
Come whispering through the ages
And thundering through the world.

Challenge me and change me,
comfort me and calm me.
Completely rearrange me,
Soothe me with a psalm.

Teach me how to please you,
Show me how to live.
Inspire me to praise you
For all the love you give.

For I know the thoughts that I think toward you, said the Lord, thoughts of peace, and not of evil, to give you an expected end.

Jeremiah 29:11

There is in your grace, God of second chances, insufficient evidence to prove my latest setback is a failure. Even if it is, with you, failure is never final but an opportunity to learn and grow. When I goof, as I am prone to do, help me from doubling the problem by failing to take advantage of your redemption.

O God, you have called each of us to special tasks, purposes, and vocations, equipping us with the skills and energy to perform them. For some, our vocations send us into the labor force; for some, it is soon bringing retirement. For some, it is in full-time homemaking. For some, our vocations are in artistic skills; for some, in volunteering, helping, neighboring. Always, there is that first call from you, God of vision, working through our work to help, heal, change a needful world.

Remember the past, and learn from its mistakes.
Honor the present, and make each moment count.
Dream the future, and work hard to make the dream come true.

Create in me a clean heart, O God;
and renew a right spirit within me.

Psalm 51:10

When the winds of life blow,
I'll hang onto myself.
When the road forks in two,
I'll be true to myself.
When the going gets rough,
I'll have faith in myself.
When the journey gets long,
I'll believe in myself.

The strongest principle of growth lies in the human choice.

—George Eliot

Tossing leaves onto a fire, we name them as regrets and failures from which we choose to be free. We trust you to redeem even these, our deadest moments. They, like autumn leaves, can make the brightest blaze.

Stir new possibilities into life from the embers; fan the sparks of dreams so that we may become one with your purpose for us. It is the root from which we, leaf and human life, begin and from which the most amazing new creation can burst into being, a flame in the darkness.

The mind is like a garden of fertile soil into which the seeds of our thoughts, ideas, and intentions are planted. With loving care and nurturing attention, those seeds bloom forth to manifest in our lives as wonderful opportunities and events. Those seeds that we choose to either ignore or neglect will simply die off. Thus, our mind constantly turns over old growth into new. It is where we focus our energy and give our love that breaks through the dark soil into the light of day. It then becomes the visible good in our life, casting off new seeds to one day bloom forth in a cycle of renewal and abundance.

Today I need your help, God, feeling the need for a breath of fresh air. The old habits and attitudes I've clung to for so long seem stale and worn out. Renew me from the inside out, starting now!

Making progress doesn't always mean continuing forward on the same path. It may mean retracing your steps, taking an unexpected turn, or even stopping to rest and renew your spirit.

You heard my prayers to ease my pell-mell race through life, and I am changing. Only you could teach this old dog new tricks. I feel your companionship in walks and exercise, in contemplation and prayer. I'm enjoying this new pace you set.

Dear Lord, I need renewal in my life.
But tell me what you want me to be, first,
then tell me what you want me to do.
Speak, for I am listening,
Guide, for I am willing to follow.
Be silent, for I am willing to rest in your love.

Ambition feeds the spirit just as food feeds the body, energizing the mind to think of better solutions, nourishing the soul to try just one more time, and empowering the heart to reach a little further.

Hopeful people have a peace about them, a way of looking at everything that happens as an opportunity for growth and happiness. Their lives are not any easier than anyone else's; it's their attitude that sets them apart.

Lord, today my heart goes out to all those whose past mistakes weigh them down and make any vision they have of their future dreary at best. Oh, that they might know you and the saving grace you bring! Draw near to them today, Lord. Reveal yourself to them in a way that will reach them, and through your mercy and forgiveness, bestow upon them a new vision—a new hope.

Lord, so often we find ourselves asking you to save us from bad situations only to discover you quietly revealing to us that we are our own worst enemies! Teach us to break destructive habits and to stop polluting our minds with negative thoughts, Lord. Save us from our enemies, even when it means you have to step in and save us from ourselves!

When I'm bored, remind me:
This is the excitement of life—
darkness alternating with light,
down dancing with up,
and inactivity being absolutely essential
—as prelude—to the most fulfilling
experiences of all.

God Almighty, please help me to put everything into perspective. I want to be realistic but also optimistic. Please send me hope and give me strength of mind to make things right again. Amen.

God, I ask in prayer that you help me hold the vision of a better world, and that I may clearly know my role in making that better world a reality. Let my vision join that of others, to create a more joyful world for those who come after us. Amen.

Lord, thank you for being a God of new beginnings. Give me a fresh start today as I trust in you. Amen.

This week, give me the wisdom to see my own imperfections clearly and the strength to transform them for the better.

Do not look back and agonize over roads not taken, dreams not pursued. Instead, look ahead to the future to new roads to discover and new dreams to fulfill.

Lord,
I like the part about "new" and "better,"
But what's that going to look like? Feel like?
What's all this going to mean?
I want transformation,
But the change part scares me.
Give me strength, Lord.
Help me accept your gift of new life.
Lead me forward.
I put my trust in you.
Amen.

Lord, sometimes I get frustrated, especially when I have to face something new. Thank you for giving me an open heart. Help me accept change and rejoice in new experiences and new people. Help me to be grateful for new opportunities and always see the good things even when I am afraid to try something new.

Today I want to spend time with you, Renewing Spirit.
In fact, I'd like to spend the whole day just being
in your presence.
For this one day I will not worry about the work I
have to do or the goals I want to accomplish.
I will pull back and simply listen for your guidance.
I'm willing to change my life in order to fit your
perfect will, and I ask that you begin that work in
my heart, even now.
I'll let go of personal ambition, for now.
I'll loosen my grip on the things I've wanted to
accomplish and the recognition I've craved for so long.
All of this I give over to you.
I'm content to be a servant for now, quiet and
unnoticed, if that is what you desire.
I'm even willing to be misunderstood, if you will only
respond to my sincere prayer for a renewed heart.
Thank you. I need you so much.

So here I am, waiting. I have answered your call to pray. I have heard your guidance—to sit tight. I have chosen quiet and rest because that is your will for me now. I am sitting on the sidelines, watching the hectic pace around me. I am finding contentment in the little blessings that flow into my days. I am trying to see all these things as big blessings because they come from you. But when can I get going again? When will I do the great works I've envisioned? When will the situation require dedicated action once again? When will I hear the trumpet call? When will I finally move onward and upward? I'm ready Great Spirit! Here I am . . . waiting.

When we awaken the sleeping lion of potential within, we allow it to spring forth in our lives with a mighty, joyful roar.

I will not let the pessimists of the world squelch my belief that what I do can make a difference. I am determined to maintain my inspiration to change the world in whatever small ways I can.

In this time of change, help me to be patient, God. Let me not run ahead of you and your plans. Give me courage to do only what is before me and to keep my focus on my responsibilities. I am tempted to daydream about the future; however, the future is in your hands.

Thus, may I be close to you in all my thoughts, accomplish the task before me today, and do it with all my heart.

Father, it stings when the ones I love correct me. I don't like to be wrong or feel like I'm being criticized. But that's just wounded pride revealing itself. Deep down I appreciate learning the truth so

I can learn and grow. Flattery feels nice in the moment, but it doesn't do much real good. People who risk hurting me because they love me are the ones I should listen to. Help me get over my wounded pride quickly and move on in light of what I've learned. And bless those who care enough for me to speak the truth in love.

Spirit of God, keep teaching me the ways of change and growth. Like the wind, you cannot be tracked or traced. The breezes blow where they will: silently, invisibly, with great power. Just as you are working in lives even now. Let me know your calling as you move in me! Yes, whisk with your persistent prompting through all the windows of my soul, the dark corners of my heart.

O Lord, let me not live to be useless.

—John Wesley

Lord, help us not to be stubborn. We want our broken hearts to heal. Amen.

Teach me, teach me, dearest Jesus
In thine own sweet loving, way,
All the lessons of perfection
I must practice day by day.
Teach me meekness, dearest Jesus,
Of Thine own the counterpart;
Not in words and actions only,
But the meekness of the heart.
Teach, Humility, sweet Jesus
To this poor, proud heart of mine,
Which yet wishes, O my Jesus,
To be modeled after Thine.

—Reverend F. X. Lasance

Lord, make me an instrument of your peace;
where there is hatred, let me sow love;
where there is injury, pardon;
where there is doubt, faith;
where there is despair, hope;
where there is darkness, light;
and where there is sadness, joy.
Divine Master, grant that I may not so much
seek to be consoled as to console;
to be understood as to understand;
to be loved as to love.
For it is in giving that we receive,
it is in pardoning that we are pardoned,
and it is in dying that we are born to eternal life.

—St. Francis of Assisi

Open up my heavy heart,
That surely day by day,
The bitterness and wrath in me
Will slowly drain away.
God let your spirit enter in
And fill each empty space
With peace and healing to my soul
Through your unending grace.

God Almighty, please help me to put everything into perspective. I want to be realistic but also optimistic. Please send me hope and give me strength of mind to make things right again. Amen.

Your changes touch my life with hope and mystery. God of love and power, I come today ready and eager to experience your power working through me.

Protect us all and keep us safe,
Help us find our way.
Show us light and make us wise,
Keep the wolves at bay.
Help us not put our trust in doors and locks
and shrill alarms,
Help us rest in angels' strong and ever-present arms.

Thank you, God, for the wisdom to know when to speak, what to say, and how to say it. Guard my mouth today from any form of foolishness, that in all circumstances I might honor you with my words.

Chapter 8

Family

And will be a father unto you, and ye shall be my sons and daughters, saith the Lord Almighty.

2 Corinthians 6:18

Be kind to your little children, Lord.
Be a gentle teacher, patient with our
weakness and stupidity.
And give us the strength and
discernment to do what you tell us,
and so grow in your likeness.
May we all live in the peace that
comes from you.
May we journey towards your city,
sailing through the waters of sin
untouched by the waves,
borne serenely along by the Holy Spirit.
Night and day may we give you praise
and thanks, because you have
shown us that all things belong to you,
and all blessings are gifts from you.
To you, the essence of wisdom, the
foundation of truth, be glory for
evermore.

—Clement of Alexandria

And thy seed shall be as the dust of the earth, and thou shalt spread abroad to the west, and to the east, and to the north, and to the south: and in thee and in thy seed shall all the families of the earth be blessed.

Genesis 28:14

There is a choice, O God, when I spot the crayon markings on the wall, the spilled food, the wet towel on the bed. I have equal breath to scream or laugh. I feel the tickle of my funny bone and know which choice you want me to make. Join us as we laugh our way into a better mood.

If one perfect day were created by me,
These are the things I would most want to see:
Sun in the morning and moonbeams at night,
Birds singing sweetly, then fluttering from sight,
The whispering wind as it passes my face,
The fragrance of baking so sweet to the taste,
Blossoming flowers with shimmering dew,
The sound of the brook as the water roars through,
A kiss from the people that love me the most,
Tender embraces that snuggle me close,
Smiles from kind strangers just walking by,
The sound of a new born babe's gurgles and sighs,
Proud eyes of a grandmother walking with grace,
An old man with memories that show in his face,
My angel that watches and guards from above,
The laughter of children and, mostly, their love.

Let me not turn away from the oppressed, the needy, Lord, in order to "protect" the children. Instead, nudge me to enlist them with the invitation to help find solutions that we can do as a family. In this way they learn that they, too, can make a difference.

Dear God, thank you for children who teach us to be open and forgiving. Help us forgive those who hurt us so the pain will not be passed on through the generations. Thank you for forgiving our sins and help us be at peace with our families. Amen.

Heavenly Father, we are thankful for family. Please bring our family together in happiness. Help us see everything as your children do: with wonder and awe. Glorious are your creations! Thank you for creating us. We love our family. We love you. Amen.

Lord, look down upon my family with merciful eyes, and help us to heal the divides that threaten to grow between us. Guide us toward the solutions that will empower everyone involved, and remind us that we work better when we work together. Help us to speak honestly with each other. Amen.

As a child, you followed behind your mother and copied her every move. As a teenager, you raced in front of her because you knew all the answers. As an adult, you walk beside her because she is your friend.

The warmth of a genuine hug can send the spirit soaring.

Those earliest recollections can be fuzzy, but impressions clear as snapshots come easily into focus: the lap where you always felt secure; the shoulder where you snuggled for comfort; the hand that clasped yours and guided you into the world.

A lullaby is simply a parent's love set to music.

If you ask the most accomplished people in the world what is most important to them, they will all give the same answer: family. The love and devotion of family serves as the foundation upon which dreams are built. The support of family acts as wings, which each member can use to fly to new heights of achievement. The honesty and trustworthiness of family creates a sanctuary that can be depended upon in times of struggle and discouragement. The blessings of family bolster the spirit. The pride of family enthuses the heart. With a loving family standing behind you, it becomes much easier to stand on your own.

I want to give everything to you, my sweet child: spring's dewy raindrops, summer's soft warmth, autumn's gentle briskness, winter's cool beauty...all the seasons of a richly woven life.

I have such good intentions, Lord of promise, but sometimes I slip as I am carrying them out. Guide my actions so that they match my words as I make firm footprints for my children to follow. Make me worthy of being their pathfinder. Amen.

At every step the child should be allowed to meet the real experiences of life; the thorns should never be plucked from his roses.

—Ellen Key

"Family" means more than just the people who share your bloodline. You need not live in the same house or grow up with the same last name in order be a family. The only requirement is a bond of love and support.

No custom is more pleasant than getting to know each other around the dinner table.

May you know the joy of giving in this family. Not only on birthdays and holidays, but every day. Not only when others are looking, but when no one will ever find out. Give, and give again! For this is the only true route to happiness, the only road to lasting peace.

Someday I hope to do for you what you've always done for me. I'll be the one you turn to for help, the shoulder you cry on, the confidante with whom you share your secrets. My dream is to take care of you the way you've always taken care of me.

Train up a child in the way he should go: and when he is old, he will not depart from it.

Proverbs 22:6

I am your child.
Your vision created me.
Your dream manifested itself in me.
Your hope molded me.
Your love breathed life into me.

Bless this gathering of what, at first glance, looks like mismatched parts, encircling God, for we want to become a family. Guide us as we step closer to one another, but not so close as to crowd. Heal wounds from past events that made this union possible.

Bless the children with the courage to try new relatives, new traditions, new homes. Empower them in their anger, helping them know that it is okay and that tears are healing. Assure them that they have the strength to live in two worlds and hearts big enough to love others. Make us, the step-adults, worthy of this love, for it comes at great cost. Help us respect previous traditions and loves and not step too close in our need to belong. For even in the midst of celebrating, there is mourning.

Look to grandmas for
a little extra help,
a little extra nudge,
a little more advice,
and a lot of extra love.

Moms always see the best in you,
No matter what you say or do.

What a joyful noise is the sound of children playing! Thank you for the chance to play with my children, to be silly with them, and to enter their world and share their zest for life. Thank you for allowing me to be young again as I share their joy and their imagination. Thank you for the gift of having a child's joy.

Though we may not choose our family members we eventually come to the understanding that someone far wiser chose them for us. Each family member has something special to teach us, whether it be forgiveness, tolerance, or acceptance. Some members give us nothing but love. Some give us nothing but grief. It is the former we often embrace, yet it is the latter from which we have the most to learn.

As you rush headlong through life, thinking always of making the next leap or rounding the next bend, Mother urges you to slow down.

It's not that she isn't eager for you to get where you're going, she just doesn't want to see you miss anything along the way.

Mothers delight in seeing something of themselves in their daughters. A greater joy, however, comes from glimpsing someone completely new and fascinating.

The just man walketh in his integrity: his children are blessed after him.

Proverbs 20:7

No man can possibly know what life means, what the world means, until he has a child and loves it. And then the whole universe changes and nothing will ever again seem exactly as it seemed before.

—Lafcadio Hearn

A family's love is as sure as the taste of an orange, as certain as the flow of water toward the sea, as familiar as the fragrance of a rose even after the bloom has faded, and as steadfast as the warmth of the sun.

Our families suffer, too, O God, as illness runs its course. Faces show strain from trying not to worry; voices sound too bright from unshed tears. Strengthen them for the grueling task that awaits; their support is life-sustaining.

Bless our homes, dear God, that we cherish the daily bread before there is none, discover each other before we leave on our separate ways, and enjoy each other for what we are, while we have time to do so.

—A Prayer from Hawaii (adapted)

Like potpourri, the unique individual "ingredients" of a family make a wondrous mixture, stirred as it is by God's enduring hand of possibilities.

Dear God, from whom every family receives its true name, I pray for all the members of my family; for those who are growing up, that they may increase in wisdom and love; for those facing changes, that they may meet them with hope; for those who are weak, that they may find strength; for those with heavy burdens, that they may carry them lightly; for those who are old and frail, that they may grow in faith.

—Anonymous

Honour thy father and thy mother: that thy days may be long upon the land which the Lord thy God giveth thee.

Exodus 20:12

Bless my family, Lord. They are a gift from you, evidence of your unwillingness for me to be alone. Until I see you face to face, may the faces of those I love be to me as your own.

What a blessing, Almighty One, to be able to earn a living for the family! To be free of worry about what they will eat, or what they will wear, or where they will sleep. You have given us so much: house, flowers, table and chairs, even a video camera to help us remember these days that are flying by so quickly. Yes, you have given. And your gifts are a serious calling: Show us how to give in return!

Your family may be less than ideal, but they are your family. It was more than luck or biology that brought you together, and you'll need more than these to keep you together. Faith and forgiveness, kindness and cooperation, laughter and love—these will preserve the precious bonds between you.

Enter and bless this family, Lord, so that its circle will be where quarrels are made up and relationships mature, where failures are forgiven and new direction found.

It is good, dear God, to be a part of this family: circle of love, place of rest, bastion of peace. When every other source of comfort fails, this is where I return. Thank you for being in our midst.

Bless mother and father, sister and brother, grandpa and grandma, uncle and aunt, and all the cousins. Here we are in your sight, this family: May we please you, day by day.

May you find joy and satisfaction in your family life: in building a home and setting up a residence—be blessed! in finding a job and working diligently—be blessed! in taking care of little ones and making friends in the neighborhood—be blessed! in seeking God for all your help and guidance, bringing every care to him, yes, I pray, may you indeed be blessed.

My son, hear the instruction of thy father, and forsake not the law of thy mother.

Proverbs 1:8

Parents lend children their experience and a vicarious memory; children endow their parents with a vicarious immortality.

—George Santayana

As I watched the seasons change, I saw each falling leaf, every crystal snowflake, every budding blossom with new amazement...for I watched it all through your wondrous eyes.

Beat upon mine, little heart! beat! beat!
Beat upon mine! you are mine, my sweet!
All mine from your pretty blue eyes to
your feet, my sweet!

—Alfred, Lord Tennyson

You give me a million reasons to glow with pride.

Progress, in the folds of a family, O God, is not a straight, flat line but rather ups and downs. Like squiggles on a heart monitor, they merely chart the daily rhythm of life. Give me energy and patience to go with the flow.

How to weather life: Share your sunny disposition, your bright smile, and your breezy welcome with everyone you meet.

Love children especially, for like the angels they too are sinless, and they live to soften and purify our hearts, and as it were, to guide us.

—Feodor Dostoevsky

Enter and bless this family, Lord, so that its circle will be where quarrels are made up and relationships mature; where failures are forgiven and new directions found.

But if any provide not for his own, and specially for those of his own house, he hath denied the faith, and is worse than an infidel.

1 Timothy 5:8

Bless all that happens here, O God, planner and builder. May we find laughter and love and strength and sanctuary. Bless all who visit our love-built home, family and companions with whom we can grow. May we, like you, offer shelter and welcome.

To be alone and in pain is so much worse than being surrounded by friends and family who care.

Your mother remembers times when you were almost perfect, as well as times when you were anything but, and she loves you all the more for both.

Guide me, O God, to savor today and all that is yet to be discovered at the hands of my children. I know that what came before and what is yet to be form a marvelous mosaic of the whole.

Bless us in this time of play together. Let each child know he or she is loved. And let us parents recognize that the love we offer here is the same affection you have already worked in our own hearts.

Visiting with family is like rereading favorite books. Though you know the stories by heart, you are compelled to turn the pages again and again, reliving the precious memories one more time.

Taking part in family traditions is such a joyous experience! Today I will take time to recall the traditions I experienced as a child and the family times I shared with those around me. I am grateful for those memories and for the opportunity to share those traditions with my family and friends today. Continuing a tradition feels like taking joyful steps along a path from the past to the future.

We come today, O God, as near strangers gathered from scattered lives, for families no longer live close by. Be the common thread running through our reuniting as we recall and rededicate our ancestors' memory.

Through this meal and catching up, embrace us and send us back to our distant homes renewed, refreshed, and revitalized until we once again join hands with you around the family table.

Creating a family is like a building coming to life on graph paper, line by line, wall by wall, space by space. In the construction, make sure there are doors that swing both ways.

Thanks for being there during the good times—parties and birthdays and special occasions. Thank you even more for being there in the bad times. What would I do without you?

God setteth the solitary in families: he bringeth out those which are bound with chains: but the rebellious dwell in a dry land.

Psalm 68:6

What's love like? It's like this: Being loved will make you feel light enough to fly up and out into the world. Loving someone will help you find your way home again.

Chapter 9

Friendship

A friend loveth at all times, and a brother is born for adversity.

Proverbs 17:17

Companion, confidante, buddy, and pal, perpetual miracle sent from above. I thank God each day for the gift of an angel, beautiful blessing of friendship and love.

Lord, I often pray for others when I need to pray with others. Show me the power of shared prayer as I meet with others in your name and in your presence. Amen.

If life has introduced you to even one person you can call a true friend, you are truly blessed.

And Elijah said unto Elisha, Tarry here, I pray thee; for the Lord hath sent me to Bethel. And Elisha said unto him, As the Lord liveth, and as thy soul liveth, I will not leave thee. So they went down to Bethel.

2 Kings 2:2

Dear God, your love embraces me like the warmth of the sun, and I am filled with light. Your hope enfolds me in arms so strong, I lack for nothing. Your grace fills me with the strength I need to move through this day. For these gifts you give me, of eternal love, eternal peace, and most of all, for eternal friendship, I thank you God.

The world's greatest treasure is the small, simple pleasure of spending our time with good friends. Amidst laughter and tears we are bound through the years by a loyalty that never ends.

A good friend makes you feel like the brightest star in the sky, the boldest color in a rainbow, the sweetest flower in a garden. She finds the best in you and brings it out for everyone else to see.

And as ye would that men should do to you, do ye also to them likewise.

Luke 6:31

Dear God, shine through me and help me lighten another's darkness by showing the same friendship that you extended. Show me a person that is in desperate need of a friend today. Help me to be sensitive, caring, and willing to go out of my way to meet this person's need right now, whether it be emotional, physical, or spiritual. Thank you that when I need a friend, you are the friend that sticketh closer than a brother. In Jesus' name, Amen.

A friend is one who understands
Any loss or gain.
A friend is one who knows your thoughts,
And whose feelings will remain.
A friend is one who encourages you,
And supports all your decisions,
A friend is one who yearns with you,
And can see your grandest visions.
A friend is one who helps you through,
Those long and stressful days.
A friend is one who lifts you up,
In a hundred different ways.
A friend is one who loves you much,
Just the way you are.
A friend is one who's in your heart,
Whether near to you or far.

What is a good friend, but a column to lean on when times are tough?
What is a good friend, but a shoulder to cry on when things are really rough?
What is a good friend, but a cheerleader to celebrate your success?
What is a good friend, but a confidante who's seen your worst and best?
What is a good friend, but a counselor to support you in hours of strife?
What is a good friend, but a traveling mate on this road we call life?

Lord, you know better than I know myself that I am growing older, and will some day be old....

Release me from craving to straighten out everybody's affairs.... With my vast store of wisdom it seems a pity not to use it all, but you know that I want a few friends at the end.

....seal my lips on my own aches and pains—they are increasing, and my love of rehearsing this is becoming sweeter as the years go by....

Keep me reasonably sweet. I do not want to be a saint—some of them are so hard to live with—but a sour old woman is one of the crowning works of the devil.

—Anonymous

He that walketh with wise men shall be wise: but a companion of fools shall be destroyed.

Proverbs 13:20

God, help me to accept the help I need and to give up my stubborn need to control the outcome of every situation. Show me that sometimes my will is not always the best and that sometimes you send us healing angels in the form of other humans. Thank you. Amen.

Faithful are the wounds of a friend; but the kisses of an enemy are deceitful.

Proverbs 27:6

My friend and I have had a falling-out, Lord. The atmosphere is strained between us; the air is chilly. I don't know what I've said or done to cause this breach in our relationship. I only know we're both at odds. Relieve the anguish that I feel, Lord. Show me how to break the silence. Help me take the first step to mend this rift between us, then you can do the rest. Heal us with your love.

Too often we lie
when people say,
How are you?
We say, "I'm fine."
We smile, and put
on our happy face.

Why can't we be honest,
at least with loved ones,
and say, "I hurt"?
Why can't we cry honest tears
and let a friend
comfort us for a moment—
embrace us
with loving arms,
as we take off
the mask we wear
to hide the pain?

Two are better than one; because they have a good reward for their labour. For if they fall, the one will lift up his fellow: but woe to him that is alone when he falleth; for he hath not another to help him up.

Ecclesiastes 4:9–10

The love of a friend has often seemed like my life preserver, keeping me afloat in turbulent waters.

When I am weak and stumble, you give me sympathy instead of sermons. You show me mercy instead of meanness. You speak tenderly instead of tearing down my already-fragile ego. You are a true friend.

Heavenly Father, I am glad to have even just one companion, but you have sent me many more! I thank you for my friends and family. I am happy to have so many shoulders on which I can lean. Amen.

I thank you for the healing power of friends and for the positive emotions friendship brings. Thank you for sending companions to me so we can support and encourage one another and share our joys and sorrows. My friends represent for me your presence and friendship here on earth. Please keep them in your care, Father. We need each other, and we need you. Amen.

True wealth cannot be measured in material objects or wordly possessions, but in the depth and quality of our friendships.

A healthy friendship enhances our lives. What a blessing to have someone who wants to share all our joys and sorrows. We should continually strive to be the kind of friend God would like us to be—and the kind of friend that we would like to have.

It's easy to love a friend for all the things we have in common. It's harder, but much more valuable, to love the things that set us apart from one another. Learning to appreciate our differences brings a new level of intimacy to our relationships with others.

If you listen to two good friends having a conversation, it sounds like two finely tuned musical instruments—they're in perfect pitch with one another.

We pass through seasons in friendships, just as we pass through seasons of the year. Our relationships with others grow, bloom, and sometimes wilt, merely because their time has come. We don't need to regret these passings, for they are a natural part of the earth's movement. Instead, we can look at them with fond recollection, knowing that spring will soon come.

We look to our friends for different things. Some are "night-on-the-town" friends. Some are telephone friends. Some are office friends. Some are advice friends. Like colorful blossoms, each contributes her unique qualities to a huge bouquet and brings something special to our lives.

A best friend absorbs half your sadness and amplifies twice your joy.

Ointment and perfume rejoice the heart: so doth the sweetness of a man's friend by hearty counsel.

Proverbs 27:9

Friendships, like gardens, must be nourished and cultivated if they are to flourish and thrive. Take time to pull the weeds, turn the soil, and plant new seeds. Then enjoy the beauty of this love you have created.

Let me be an angel to someone today.
Let me make life easier in some important way.
Let me offer kindness as I go
and cultivate the seeds of hope
so they might bloom and grow.

Let me be a blessing to a stranger or friend.
Let me find a broken heart that I can help
to mend.
Let me offer words of love to those who
know despair
and tend to wounds of others
with compassion, hope, and care.

Let me be an angel to someone in need.
Let me be the bearer of some unexpected deed.
Let me teach the ways of love to everyone I see
and bring the gift of peace to those
who seek serenity.

Friendship is a seed planted during a chance first meeting that grows into a flower when it's watered with love. Thank you for tending our garden of friendship.

When we give thanks and praise to someone, we honor the presence of God in that person. Our gratitude for the people we love is our acknowledgment of spirit expressing through them.

The beauty of good friends is that they can spend long months away from each other, yet never grow apart.

Life may tell us that our paths should part, but God has placed you in my heart. And though I may not return to you,our friendship will remain strong and true.

Give thanks for your friends, each and every day of your life.

Wherefore comfort yourselves together, and edify one another, even as also ye do.

1 Thessalonians 5:11

A phone call from a friend—a cool drink on a parched, dry day. A letter from a friend—a break in the clouds when the rain pours down. A hug from a friend—a down-filled blanket while a snowstorm rages.

One there is, above all others,
Well deserves the name of Friend;
his is love beyond a brother's,
Costly, free, and knows no end;
They who once his kindness prove
find it everlasting love.
O for grace our hearts to soften!
Teach us, Lord, at length to love;
We, alas! forget too often
What a Friend we have above;
But when home our souls are brought,
We will love You as we ought.

—John Newton,
"One There Is, Above All Others"

When you're stuck on the ground,
friends help you fly.
When you give up,
friends tell you to try.
When all is dark,
friends show you the light.
When you stray from your path,
friends set you right.
Life has its ups and downs, it's true,
but friends will always be there for you.

Blessed are those who have found one person they can call a true friend. Doubly blessed are those with the good sense to keep that friend.

As every man hath received the gift, even so minister the same one to another, as good stewards of the manifold grace of God.
If any man speak, let him speak as the oracles of God; if any man minister, let him do it as of the ability which God giveth: that God in all things may be glorified through Jesus Christ, to whom be praise and dominion for ever and ever. Amen

1 Peter 4:10–11

The best medicine for a discouraged spirit is a dose of love. Add a touch of support from friends and family, mix with a pinch of awareness of God's presence, and spread over your entire heart and soul. Wait ten seconds, then smile. Nothing can withstand such a powerful healing balm.

Hold on tight to your friends; they are one of God's great blessings.

The stars come nightly to the sky;
The tidal wave unto the sea;
Nor time, nor space, nor deep, nor high
Can keep my own away from me.

Friendship is the triple alliance of the three great powers, Love, Sympathy, and Help.

My friends have come to me unsought; the great God gave them to me.

—Ralph Waldo Emerson

When it comes to words of wisdom,
on these you can depend:
No matter where life takes you,
it's better with a friend.

Just one seemingly simple act of kindness can have far-reaching consequences. If we stop to help someone out, we might make their day—or even make a new friend.

It is my joy in life to find
At every turning of the road
The strong arm of a comrade kind
To help me onward with my load.
And since I have no gold to give,
And love alone must make amends,
My only prayer is, while I live—
God make me worthy of my friends.

—Frank Dempster Sherman

Thank God for friendship. It brings us joy and comfort and provides refuge from an often harsh world.

There is a fine line between helping each other person and making them dependent on us. We can help a bird with a broken wing by wrapping the injury, but we cannot make that bird fly. That is up to the bird. We can support a friend who wants to go after dream, but we cannot go after that dream for them. That is up to our friend. To truly help another person, we need to guide them to help themselves. Then, and only then, will they be able to become healed, whole, and empowered.

Someone to lean on when times get too tough,
someone to laugh with at life's silly stuff,
someone who'll share when there's
more than enough,
that's what a friend means to me.

One of the best things you can say to a friend is simply, "I'll be there for you." Nothing to do, nothing to prove, just the assurance of your presence when they need you. That's exactly what God tells us time and time again in the Bible. He will be there for us.

We didn't exactly see eye to eye
As our friendship teetered and years rolled by.
But thanks to the fences you'd always mend
I'm lucky today that you call me friend.

Friendships are the golden threads woven into the tapestries of our lives.

A friend loves you at all times. When you aren't looking your best, a friend insists that you do. When you don't feel your best, a friend makes you laugh.

When we love our friends, we see their goodness and beauty, no matter what they look like, how old they are, what they choose to wear. When we learn to recognize the soul underneath these outward trappings, our own lives are enriched.

Visiting with old friends is like rereading favorite books. Though you know the stories by heart, you are compelled to turn the pages again and again, reliving the precious memories one more time.

A true friend gives the best advice: not necessarily what you want to hear, but what you need to know.

A friend's smile can warm the winter sky and entice the sun to stay a little longer.

But friendship is precious, not only in the shade, but in the sunshine of life; and thanks to a benevolent arrangement of things, the greater part of life is sunshine.

—Thomas Jefferson

I sound much better when I'm singing with my friends, I kick much higher when I'm dancing with my friends, and I laugh much longer when I'm laughing with my friends.

Oh, the comfort—the inexpressible comfort of feeling safe with a person—having neither to weigh thoughts nor measure words, but pouring them all right out, just as they are, chaff and grain together; certain that a faithful hand will take them and sift them, keep what is worth keeping, and then with the breath of kindness blow the rest away.

—Dinah Maria Mulock Craik

Friendships come about by good fortune, mutual respect, and the grace of God.

That is, that I may be comforted together with you by the mutual faith both of you and me.

Romans 1:12

You are forever changed when you find a true friend.

A true friend laughs at your best funny story no matter how many times she's heard it.

The miracle of friendship usually begins with a simple smile.

I'd like a little money.
I'd like a little ease.
But a friendship that is faithful
Can outweigh both of these.

Instead of a gem or a flower, cast the gift of a lovely thought into the heart of a friend.

—George MacDonald

Barren trees and a chill in the air cannot dispel the warmth among friends.

Give to your friends unselfishly and freely, and expect nothing in return but their friendship.

Make no friendship with an angry man; and with a furious man thou shalt not go:
Lest thou learn his ways, and get a snare to thy soul.
Be not thou one of them that strike hands, or of them that are sureties for debts.
If thou hast nothing to pay, why should he take away thy bed from under thee?

Proverbs 22:24–27

It is not good to be alone—even in Paradise.

—Yiddish folk saying

Kind words and thoughtful deeds are celebrated year-round among friends.

Sweet is the memory of distant friends! Like the mellow rays of the departing sun, it falls tenderly, yet sadly, on the heart.

—Washington Irving

Well, the winter's gone, and I've written no books, earned no fortune; but I've made a friend worth having and I'll try to keep him all my life.

—Louisa May Alcott

So long as we love we serve; so long as we are loved by others, I would almost say that we are indispensable; and no man is useless while he has a friend.

—Robert Louis Stevenson

Friends like you are a rare treasure. Thank you for all you've done.

Chapter 10

Hardships & Healing

Be strong and of a good courage, fear not, nor be afraid of them: for the Lord thy God, he it is that doth go with thee; he will not fail thee, nor forsake thee.

Deuteronomy 31:6

Take this burden from me, Lord,
Free me from this pain.
Let me move with ease and grace
And walk in health again.
Take this yoke upon you, Lord,
And help me toward my goal,
I'm tired of being sick and tired
And long to be made whole.
Release me from my illness
And restore me to my best.
If you can do that for me, Lord,
I'll take care of the rest.

Fear thou not; for I am with thee: be not dismayed; for I am thy God: I will strengthen thee; yea, I will help thee; yea, I will uphold thee with the right hand of my righteousness.

Isaiah 41:10

Enliven my imagination, God of new life, so that I can see through today's troubles to coming newness. Surround me with your caring so that I can live as if the new has already begun.

I am still moving, God, through storms. By your grace—over rough country, you have carried me; amidst pounding waves, you have held me; beyond the horizon of my longings you have shown me your purposes. Even in this small room, sitting still, I am moving, God. Closer.

My Creator, blessed is your presence. For you and you alone give me power to walk through dark valleys into the light again. You and you alone give me hope when there seems no end to my suffering. You and you alone give me peace when the noise of my life overwhelms me. I ask that you give this same power, hope, and peace to all who know discouragement, that they, too, may be emboldened and renewed by your everlasting love. Amen.

God, I look around my community today and I feel helpless. The homeless, the hurting, the needs each one represents are more than I can handle. But you can do it. You can meet each need. Teach me. Strengthen me and use me to serve as I reach out to my neighbor and meet Just One Need at a Time!

When I feel my control and resolve slipping, Lord, I know I only have to call on you for encouragement, direction, and guidance to get your loving assistance.

But the end of all things is at hand: be ye therefore sober, and watch unto prayer.
And above all things have fervent charity among yourselves: for charity shall cover the multitude of sins.

1 Peter 4:7–8

Lord, I need you here in the midst of this difficult situation, that the very warmth of your love will bring about the resolution and that the brightness of your light will cast out all shadows between us. Amen.

It takes great courage to heal, Lord, great energy to reach out from this darkness to touch the hem of your garment and ask for healing. Bless the brave voices telling nightmare tales of dreadful wounds to the gifted healers of this world. Together, sufferers and healers are binding up damaged parts and laying down burdens carried so long.

Dear God, you have sustained me through my illness. You have nursed my injury. You are my true physician, and I glorify your name with all my heart. Amen.

God is our refuge and strength, a very present help in trouble.

Psalm 46:1

God of my heart, I am a broken person. I do not know how to handle this suffering. I am not strong enough to do it alone. Be my strength, God, and do for me what I simply cannot do for myself. Be the glue that binds the pieces of my shattered soul back together, that I may rise and step back onto the joyful path of life again. Amen.

Of the many ways to suffer, I feel all of them in this firestorm of sadness. It robs my sleep, saps my strengh, and changes me so much I hardly recognize myself. Ease my misery, Lord. Clear my mind as though washing streaks from a window. Hold me when I cry, releasing feelings that keep me sick; send others to hold me, too. Remind me that this pain is temporary and can be relieved, just like my worries.

Sitting here in this waiting room, O God, time drags and fear festers. Remake worry into energized, active prayers, into trust in the process of healing and recovery. We're scooting over to make room for you, a companion for the waiting.

Why is there so much pain in the world, God? It's so hard to understand. Lord, help us through it all. Help us comprehend or at least simply trust in you.

I sought the Lord, and he heard me, and delivered me from all my fears.

Psalm 34:4

Dear God, the pain is so great and unbearable that I feel as though another moment of it will tear me apart. Please rescue me from this pain. Touch my body and heal me. Hear my pleas for only you have the power to deliver me from my affliction. Have mercy upon me. I cry out to you day and night, and I will turn to no one but you.

Dear Lord, each night the news is full of trouble. So much pain and sorrow. It makes me ache to see it all. Some nights, it seems that's all there is; this world seems sometimes so weary and heavy laden. Then I turn to you and know that you are nearest on the darkest days. And there is comfort in knowing you and that you have not forsaken us or the people whose world is presently dark. Amen.

Thank you, Lord, for helping us through our hard times. You have shown your love for us and made us more compassionate people. Help us show the same love to others who are going through hard times.

My grief feels as if it will never subside, God. Every thing within me melts like wax when I wake up in the morning and realize all over again what has happened. My life is forever changed. Sometimes I wonder if you are there, but I know you have promised always to be with me. Please hold me close. Amen.

Help me grieve and go on...go on in new ways you will reveal to me, Lord, as I make my faltering way as far as I can. Hold me while I name and mourn all I have lost, weeping and wailing like the abandoned child I feel I am. Then, in time and with you to lean on, I can focus on what I have left.

God of my heart, bring me comfort and peace in this time of confusion and sorrow. Help me to know that, although things are bleak, there is always a brighter tomorrow.

Give to the winds thy fears
Hope and be undismayed;
God hears thy sighs and counts thy tears
God shall lift up thy head.
Through waves and clouds and storms,
He gently clears thy way.
Wait thou his time; so shall this night
Soon end in joyous day.
Let us in life, death,
They steadfast truth declare
And publish with our latest breath
Thy love and guardian care.

—Paul Gerhardt, translated by John Wesley

Casting all your care upon him;
for he careth for you.

1 Peter 5:7

Lord, although we are often not certain of your intentions when you present us with unpleasant circumstances, we understand that you do have a reason. The hurt isn't just to spite us. Please help us to keep our outlooks positive and allow us to aid others who are as dismayed and in just as much pain as we are. Amen.

Father, you will help us to survive the seasons of surprises in our lives. For just as the harshest winter always gives way to the warm blush of spring, the season of our suffering will give way to a brighter tomorrow, where change becomes a catalyst for new growth and spiritual maturity. Amen.

God, I pray to you today for the healing that only your love can bring. I long to be free from pain and suffering, to be whole again in body, mind, and spirit. Give to me the soothing balm of your tender, loving care that I might mount up on wings of eagles and fly without pain again. Amen.

I have set the Lord always before me: because he is at my right hand, I shall not be moved.

Psalm 16:8

Creator God, you have come to me with healing in your hand. When I cried out, you heard me. You provided me with a gift that brought both peace and pleasure to my harried life. You helped me to focus on life instead of illness and sorrow. Lord, thank you for this wondrous gift. Amen.

Heal me, O Lord.
Heal my heart, my soul, my body.
Heal anything in me that is wounded, less than whole.
Then guide me to live in a way that brings healing to others, too.

Comfort, dear God, those whose eyes are filled with tears and those whose backs are near breaking with the weight of a heavy burden. Heal those whose hearts hold a wound and whose faith has been dealt a blow. Bless all who mourn and who despair. Help those who can't imagine how they'll make it through another day. For your goodness and mercy are enough for all the troubles in the world. Amen.

And he said, My presence shall go with thee, and I will give thee rest.

Exodus 33:14

Lord, this healing process is sometimes slow, and I get discouraged and filled with doubt. Can I take this? Will I make it? Yet you always remind me of your powerful presence and assure me that where I am unable to go, you will go for me and what I am unable to do by myself, you will do for me. Thank you, Lord. Amen.

Lord, I know that part of life is loss and that without loss we cannot treasure the new blessings that come our way. But I am still hurting, and the pain is deep. Help me see the beautiful silver lining that surrounds the dark clouds now hanging overhead. Amen.

When each heartbeat hurts and each breath aches, I pray, God, that you will take some of my blinding pain away. Lift me out of my pain, and give me peace. Amen.

Lord, you do not leave us to suffer alone. You are with us in pain, in sickness, and in our worst moments. Thank you for your comfort and healing power. Thank you for getting us through when our bodies fail, when our health falters, and when we need you most of all. Amen.

O Father, I feel my heart panic. I am so afraid because my world seems to be in such horrible jeopardy. Help me turn to you for courage during this dreadful time. Increase my faith and strengthen my confidence in your care for my welfare. This I pray. Amen.

But they that wait upon the Lord shall renew their strength; they shall mount up with wings as eagles; they shall run, and not be weary; and they shall walk and not faint.

Isaiah 40:31

While I wait for this piercing pain of loneliness to pass, Great Comforter, cradle me as the wailing, lost child I've become. Closing my eyes and breathing deeply, I feel your warming presence as a blanket tossed around my shoulders and know that no matter how lost I feel right now, you hold the most important truth, whispering it now: "You are my beloved child. I am with you."

Heavenly Father, you say that you will heal me. Please help me realize there are different forms of healing. While your healing is sometimes miraculous and other times almost common and everyday, your healing in on occasion invisible. These are moments when life doesn't seem to change, and I have to look inside to find a place of acceptance. It is in this place where I am reminded that who I am is separate from the pain that invades my life. Please help me to turn my thoughts to you. Amen.

O God, healing is going so-o-o-o slowly, and I am impatient and grumpy. Mind, body, or soul, this could take a long time. Remind me that recovery is a journey, not a hasty jet-lagged arrival. Bless me with faith to sustain me, step by small step. You do miraculous things with faith as tiny as mustard seeds that, in time, blossom into awesome growth. I hold that picture as I make mustard-seed progress along the road to healing.

So shall they fear the name of the Lord from the west, and his glory from the rising of the sun. When the enemy shall come in like a flood, the Spirit of the Lord shall lift up a standard against him.

Isaiah 59:19

I don't want to do it all today, Lord. I want to leave undone that which fails to serve you, and leave unsaid that which fails to glorify you.

Loving Jesus, Healer of the Sick, I place in your hands myself and all who need your healing. Help us crave the healing that only you can give. May we not define what that healing should be, but accept your gift of abundant life however you give it to us. In your way, in your time, restore us to full health and wholeness. Amen.

Lord, only you can comfort us when we grieve. The heaviness we feel at such times can make even breathing a struggle. But you, O Lord, stay close. You fill us with your peace and your comfort. You never let us retreat completely from your light into the darkness of despair. And finally, in your time, you restore joy to our souls. We are ever so grateful, O Great Comforter.

When disaster strikes our lives, God is our rock, and nothing can separate us from him. Indeed, nothing can separate us from his love.

When someone we love is trapped in a prison of defeat and discouragement, we can help them break free of the chains that bind them by doing these three things: supporting their deepest dreams, believing in their gifts and talents, and loving and accepting them for who they are at this very moment.

Lord, send me an angel to guide me and guard me, to lead and direct me, to comfort and hold me. Send me an angel who knows what my heart needs most and who always has the highest and best solutions to my most challenging problems. Send me an angel to walk with me through the dark and hold my hand as I tread the rocky road of life. Send me an angel soon, Lord.

May I be blessed in this suffering. May I know that you can use this thing to show me a mistaken attitude, a destructive behavior. In that way, may I be blessed in this suffering, O Lord, my God.

When life seems darkest and we feel lost and all alone, that is when we are most surrounded by angels who care for us. All we need to do is open our hearts to see them reaching out to us with love.

When grief fills my heart, Father, whether I'm feeling loss, shame, betrayal, or some other sorrow, I know it's temporary, even though at times it feels as though it will never go away. I know that your future for me is joy, and when it comes, I will not reject it. Strengthen me with your joy today, Father. I need it to lift up my soul.

Have not I commanded thee? Be strong and of a good courage; be not afraid, neither be thou dismayed: for the Lord thy God is with thee whithersoever thou goest.

Joshua 1:9

I feel an old familiar panic coming over me, Lord. Comfort me now. As I breathe deeply, fill me with the knowledge that you are present and you are in control. Thank you, Lord. Only your intervention can calm my troubled soul.

Dear Lord, we live in a broken world. We need your touch. Heal us of our prejudices, our sicknesses, our compulsions, our hatreds, and our shortsightedness. Help us to see people as you see them. For that matter, help us see ourselves as you see us. Teach us to treat life as the gift you meant it to be. Keep us safe. Make us whole. Give us love to spare and forgiveness that can only come from you. Amen.

When trouble strikes, O God, we are restored by small signs of hope found in ordinary places: friends, random kindness, shared pain and support. Help us collect them like mustard seeds that can grow into a spreading harvest of well-being.

Left alone now, we drift aimlessly like untied balloons let loose to fly helter-skelter. Yet life goes on, decisions must be made. O God, help us make up minds that won't stay still. Give us good sense to put off until tomorrow what we shouldn't try today. Reassure us this is only temporary, a brief hesitation, not a giving up; hold up a mirror for us to see a once-again clear-eyed person.

Calm me enough, O Lord, to breathe deeply and restoratively despite my racing heart, pounding headache, and generally fatigued body and mind. Prayer restores me in the presence of all that threatens to undo me, which I name to you now.

Touch and calm my turbulent emotions, God of the still waters. Whisper words to the listening ears of my soul. In hearing your voice, give me assurance beyond a shadow of a doubt that you are my companion in life, eternally.

Storms sometimes arrive in our lives with hurricane-force winds. We feel as if our hearts are caught in the vortex. But just when we think we'll be destroyed, a still, small voice appears in the eye of the storm to remind us that we are not alone.

Though we may not think there is something to gain in the depths of despair, it is only when we begin to heal that we finally see the truth.

Whatever tests in life you're facing, whether it's a challenge of relationships, finances, or your career, the loving Spirit that created you is always available to guide you into a better life.

If I'm honest with myself, I'll admit that the greatest joys in my life have sprung from the fertile grounds of suffering—but only after I have asked God to take charge of my garden of sorrow.

Remember to turn to God for help, for in him there is rescue, refuge, and peace.

And the peace of God, which passeth all understanding, shall keep your hearts and minds through Christ Jesus.

Philippians 4:7

Father in heaven, sometimes I feel anger welling up inside me, and I need to turn to you for counsel. Please stay near to me and help me to find ways to express my emotions without harming another's feelings or getting myself so upset I cannot see past my own feelings. I need to understand myself, express myself, and accept myself—all within the bounds of your teachings. Amen.

We are grateful, O God, for glimpses we are given of you during times like these. Thank you for showing us how, during raging winds, the mother cardinal refuses to move, standing like a mighty shelter over the fledglings beneath her wings. Secure us in the truth that we, the children of your heart, are likewise watched over and protected during life's storms.

God, how much longer must I stay curled up in a ball behind this large stone, seeking protection from the storm that swirls around me? I have watched the weeds bow and bend and still not break against the onslaught of the wind. God, I sense I must bend and bow in the midst of the strong forces that pummel me. Then I will find strength to endure until the morning light comes, when I will stand once again because of your help.

God, sometimes I wish I could be saved from the struggle and pain of learning things the hard way. But, Lord, that's not your plan, and I need to be willing to wait as you work gently from the inside out. Please grant me some strength in this time of uncertainty. I trust and love you. Amen.

When we see our enemies from God's perspective, compassion follows, for he has seen the sorrows in their hearts that have caused them to behave in such a manner. He longs to reach out to these people and comfort them, and he sometimes uses our hands to do it.

Submit yourselves therefore to God. Resist the devil, and he will flee from you.

James 4:7

Through the darkest days, God walks beside me and will never leave me. His presence comforts me and gives me the courage to keep going no matter what the circumstances are.

Your soul can dance though the pain is here.
Call healing music to your ear.
Spot emotion's fickle turning,
Leap in love,
Stretch hopes,
Master fear's deep strains.
Dare to dance both health and pain.
However clumsy, long, or fleeting,
We dance life well if grace is leading.

Chapter 11

Life

Jesus said unto her, I am the resurrection, and the life: he that believeth in me, though he were dead, yet shall he live:

And whosoever liveth and believeth in me shall never die. Believest thou this?

John 11:25–26

And whatsoever ye do, do it heartily, as to the Lord, and not unto men; Knowing that of the Lord ye shall receive the reward of the inheritance: for ye serve the Lord Christ.

Colossians 3:23–24

May you celebrate this day with all your heart.

Rejoice in the beauty of its light and warmth.

Give thanks for the air and grass and sidewalks.

Let gratitude for other faces flow into your soul.

And cherish the chance to work and play, to think and speak—knowing this: All simple pleasures are opportunities for praise.

Life is like a jigsaw puzzle. When you look at each individual piece, it makes little sense. But when the pieces are all put in their proper place, the end result is a beautiful image, whole and complete. Thus the individual events of your life may make little sense at the time they occur, but when viewed as part of the "big picture," they make all the sense in the world.

To be with God, there is no need to be continually in church. We may make [a chapel] of our heart wherein to return from time to time to converse with him in meekness, humility, and love. There is not in the world a kind of life more sweet and delightful than that of a continual conversation with God.

—Brother Lawrence

Nothing great was ever accomplished by sitting in the stands. In order to experience life fully, you must get into the race and risk being bumped, sidelined, and put out of commission for a while. But at least you will have tried. At least you will have dared. At least you will have dreamed.

Being in the flow of life means letting things happen in their own natural timing. When you try to force things to happen, you're met with resistance, and you run up against numerous obstacles. You end up taking detours that waste your time and energy, and your enthusiasm wanes as the task becomes more difficult. Often you end up making something happen, only to find that is wasn't what you really wanted to have happen! But if you just relax and go with the flow of life, the natural order of things takes over, and divine timing kicks into gear. Life becomes effortless, harmonious, and enjoyable, just as it was meant to be.

Life becomes much easier and more enjoyable when we know we are never alone. We always have our Higher Power to turn to for strength, hope, guidance, and renewal. God is on the job 24 hours a day, 7 days a week, 365 days a year.

And God said, Let the waters bring forth abundantly the moving creature that hath life, and fowl that may fly above the earth in the open firmament of heaven.

Genesis 1:20

One person who has mastered life is better than a thousand persons who have mastered only the contents of books, but no one can get anything out of life without God.

—Meister Eckhardt

I'm getting a crick in my neck trying to see around the bend, God of past and future. I'm wearing myself out second guessing. Teach me to live in today, needing just a small glimpse down the road. No need to borrow trouble that may not be waiting.

Life consists not in holding good cards but in playing those you hold well.

—Josh Billings

O Lord, bless our life stages, for they read like growth rings on a mighty tree: our beginnings and firsts with their excitement, newness, and anxiety; our middles, full of diligence and commitment and, yes, we confess, sometimes boredom, but also risk and derring-do; our "nexts," the harvests and reapings; the slowing down and freedom. In your hands this time can be rich and full like an overflowing cup, not a last or a final or an empty or an ending stage at all. You are an Alpha and Omega God, the parentheses between which we live, move, and have our being. Bless our comings and goings.

God may throw us a few curves in life—we may feel hassled, troubled, anxious, or uncomfortable, and not understand why our circumstances don't fit our desires. But if we trust in the wisdom of his plan, God will provide for all our needs.

Let me but live my life from year to year,
With forward face and unreluctant soul;
Not hurrying to, nor turning from, the goal;
Not mourning for the things that disappear
In the dim past, nor holding back in fear
From what the future veils; but with a whole
And happy heart, that pays its toll
To youth and age, and travels on with cheer.

–Henry Van Dyke

For the life of the flesh is in the blood: and I have given it to you upon the altar to make an atonement for your souls: for it is the blood that maketh an atonement for the soul.

Leviticus 17:11

How easily, O God of eternity, for us to assume our time is like the grains of sand on an ocean beach—vast and endless. Remind us that each of our lives is limited like the sand in the hourglass. May what we do with that sand, play in it, work in it, build our relationships, whatever, be wise use of this precious gift of living.

The world holds so many priceless things—the falling rain, a rose in bloom, the wind that sings, an oyster's pearl, the mustard seed. If we can cherish just one precious gift, our lives will be rich indeed.

Treasured memories form a basis for today's choices, and by using faith's discernment, I've learned what matters and what lasts.

Think of each problem you encounter as nothing more than a challenging reminder from God to think a little higher and reach a little farther. When met with a difficult situation along the road of life, greet it, acknowledge it, and move past it. Then you will be able to continue on your journey a little stronger, a little wiser.

Life with faith has meaning and purpose. It transforms the smallest actions into elements of significance, contributing to a better world.

Most of us realize that we are naturally self centered, and we often respond to those around us in ways that make us appear proud, haughty, or arrogant. But if we look at Jesus' life, we see an excellent example of humility—an example that we should strive to follow. He taught that pride was destructive, but humility was powerful. Rather than touting his own greatness, Jesus was willing to kneel down and wash the feet of others, to show that we should all be servants to each other—and to God.

Abide thou with me, fear not: for he that seeketh my life seeketh thy life: but with me thou shalt be in safeguard.

1 Samuel 22:23

You can reach the end of one road, but you never come to the end of the line.

When one door closes another door opens; but we often look so long and so regretfully upon the closed door that we do not see the one which has opened for us.

—Alexander Graham Bell

He asked life of thee, and thou gavest it him, even length of days for ever and ever.

Psalm 21:4

Inspired by you, Great God, and grateful for the unique gifts we're discovering, we toss ourselves into the stream of life to make ripples wherever we are. In your hands, our gifts can offer a gift that keeps on making ever-widening circles to reach all those stranded on shore.

A wise person once said to live each day as though you might die tomorrow. But you should also live each day as though you might live forever.

We make our own plans, but it is God who leads the way and clears the obstacles from our path.

When I am wrong, I turn within to find the right way. God's eternal wisdom is like a flowing river I can tap into at any time, especially when I am clueless and don't know which way to turn. I take comfort in knowing I don't have to be a genius and figure out every last detail of my life. God knows best, and as long as I stay in tune with his word, I will be divinely inspired.

Grow old along with me!
The best is yet to be,
The last of life, for which the first
was made;
Our times are in his hand
Who saith, "A whole I planned,
Youth shows but half;
trust God:
See all, nor be afraid."

—Robert Browning

One day when we face these beings of light who have guided our path and done God's work in our life, we will wonder how we ever overlooked their presence.

If you really don't miss someone or someplace, you're not living life deeply enough.

Lord, I wish to live a long life, but I fear growing old. I want to accomplish great things, but I fear risking what I already have. I desire to love with all my heart, but the prospect of self-revelation makes me shrink back. Perhaps for just this day, you would help me reach out? Let me bypass these dreads and see instead your hand reaching back to mine—right now—just as it always has.

Faith in a wise and trustworthy God, even in broken times like these, teaches us a new math: subtracting old ways and adding new thoughts because sharing with God divides our troubles and multiplies unfathomable possibilities for renewed life.

Dost thou love life? Then do not squander time; for that's the stuff life is made of.

—Benjamin Franklin

Intelligence can be measured by certificates on your wall or books you have read, but, in the end, all that knowledge pales in comparison to the wisdom gained when you truly participate in life.

Each life that touches ours for good is a reflection of God's love for us.

In a moment of quiet, dark stillness, or even in the bustle of daily life, you may occasionally feel that you are in the company of an angel. Revel in its divine presence!

O God, we give thanks that your son Jesus Christ, who has shared our earthly life, has now ascended to prepare our heavenly life. Grant that, through coming to know him by faith on earth, we may come to know him by sight in heaven.

—The Gelasian Sacramentary

I call heaven and earth to record this day against you, that I have set before you life and death, blessing and cursing: therefore choose life, that both thou and thy seed may live: That thou mayest love the Lord thy God, and that thou mayest obey his voice, and that thou mayest cleave unto him: for he is thy life, and the length of thy days: that thou mayest dwell in the land which the Lord sware unto thy fathers, to Abraham, to Isaac, and to Jacob, to give them.

Deuteronomy 30:19–20

Truth is as impossible to be soiled by any outward touch as the sunbeam.

—John Milton

When you are in the midst of suffering, time is too slow. When you are in the midst of excitement, time moves too quickly. Only in the present moment does time cease to exist. True happiness is found there, in the now, where regrets of the past and the fears of the future give way to the bliss of just being alive.

Certain days, certain events come bounding into our way to remind us of how out of control life really is. It is then that we are most grateful for the angels that guard our way and guide our paths.

The thief cometh not, but for to steal, and to kill, and to destroy: I am come that they might have live, and that they might have it more abundantly.

John 10:10

How joyful life becomes when we surrender to our faith in God, allowing his will to work through us. We give up resistance and frustration, and things suddenly seem to flow with greater ease. We still have obstacles, but also the strength and resources to overcome them. Living in faith and experiencing more peace and joy is what God intended for us!

Life is a gift to be used every day,
Not to be smothered and hidden away;
It isn't a thing to be stored in a chest
Where you gather your keepsakes and treasure your best;
It isn't a joy to be sipped now and then
And promptly put back in a dark place again.
Life is a gift that the humblest may boast of
And one that the humblest may well make the most of.
Get out and live it each hour of the day,
Wear it and use it as much as you may;
Don't keep it in niches and corners and grooves,
You'll find that in service its beauty improves.

—Edgar A. Guest

As you look at your own life, how might you be an angel to others? How might you pattern your life as to inspire others to greater heights in their own loving and giving?

God asks no man whether he will accept life. That is not the choice. You must take it. The only choice is how.

—Henry Ward Beecher

See then that ye walk circumspectly,
not as fools, but as wise,
Redeeming the time, because
the days are evil.

Ephesians 5:15–16

Faith is my soul's good friend that urges me on, convincing me I will victoriously reach the finish line in this race called my life.

There is only the gift of the moment. Savor it. It is a gift.

—Anonymous

No day should ever be so hectic that there is not time in it for solitude and reflection.

God's highest priority is that we get to know him and live a life that reflects his love and justice.

Loving Jesus is not something that happens automatically. It is not something that's easy or natural. It is learned through the trials of life.

Do all things without murmurings and disputings:

That ye may be blameless and harmless, the sons of God, without rebuke, in the midst of a crooked and perverse nation, among whom ye shine as lights in the world;

Holding forth the word of life; that I may rejoice in the day of Christ, that I have not run in vain, neither laboured in vain.

Yea, and if I be offered upon the sacrifice and service of your faith, I joy, and rejoice with you all.
For the same cause also do ye joy, and rejoice with me.

Philippians 2:14–18

Christ, the blessed one, gives to all
Wonderful words of life;
Sinner heed now his loving call,
Wonderful words of life.
All so freely given,
Wooing us to heaven:
Beautiful words, wonderful words
Wonderful words of life.

—Phillip P. Bliss